I0605463

Praise for *The Gospel After Christendom*

At a time when some say Christianity has become culturally obsolete, this book, the best introduction to cultural apologetics on the market, provides demonstrations—rational, artistic, and practical—that the story of God with and for us, the gospel of Jesus Christ, is as necessary as ever for the pursuit of truth, goodness, and beauty, the sum and substance of human flourishing in all areas of life.

—KEVIN J. VANHOOZER, research professor of systematic theology, Trinity Evangelical Divinity School

Boy, do we need this book! In an era where cultures collide and Christianity is often dismissed in many of them or worn with a facade that is not the real thing, we need an approach that is culturally aware and says the gospel is better than the variety of things currently being offered to people. These chapters point the way for all of us to accomplish the calling God gives believers to represent God well in a challenging world. It calls for boldness and care in a way that listens to others' longings and engages with a biblical response full of grace and truth. Well done.

—DARRELL L. BOCK, executive director of cultural engagement at the Hendricks Center, and senior research professor of New Testament studies at Dallas Theological Seminary

Many fellow believers are used to preaching Christ in non-Christian and anti-Christian cultures. American Christians are not. We need to be. Read this book to discover how.

—MICHAEL HORTON, J. Gresham Machen Professor of Systematic Theology and Apologetics, Westminster Seminary California

This volume brings together some of today's most creative Christian thinkers to tackle the problem of how to make the case for faith to cynical, secular Westerners who think they've already heard it all. The result is both an encouragement and a challenge to twenty-first-century believers.

—MOLLY WORTHEN, author of *Spellbound: How Charisma Shaped American History from the Puritans to Donald Trump*

Christian witness requires, among other spiritual capacities, a kind of biliteracy. We must be fluent in the truth of the Scriptures and in our cultural contexts. *The Gospel After Christendom* is an essential primer in this fluency that enables powerful gospel proclamation, and I highly recommend its collected wisdom.

—Jen Pollock Michel, author and speaker

Apologetics has perennially endeavored to persuade about the Christian hope. The best approach has been Cultural apologetics, meaning recognizing whole persons, their history, and their circumstances. This anthology introduces us in a superb manner to the need for the vindication of the Christian faith in a post-Christendom world. It a must-read for anyone concerned to explain the faith to outsiders and insiders alike in these perplexing times.

—William Edgar, professor emeritus of apologetics, Westminster Seminary

It's no secret that Christianity has receded significantly in the West. So what does faithful witness look like in this age? Collin Hansen, Skyler Flowers, and Ivan Mesa convene the brightest Christian minds to offer theologically rich, biblically faithful, and pastorally wise direction to help God's people discern the times. Neither cynical nor naive, this resource will both encourage and challenge any believer who earnestly desires revival and gospel advance. Every pastor should have this book on his shelf.

—Daniel Darling, director of the Land Center for Cultural Engagement at Southwestern Seminary, author of several books, including, *The Dignity Revolution*, *Agents of Grace*, and the forthcoming *In Defense of Christian Patriotism*

This wonderful book represents so many great things all at once: a practical handbook on evangelism, a treasure trove of both biblical and cultural insight, a powerful apologetic for cultural apologetics itself, and the fruit of the joyous collegiality we've found together at the Keller Center. I can't think of another book I'd rather have close to hand when thinking about engaging western culture with the beautiful message of Jesus Christ."

—Sam Allberry, associate pastor, Immanuel Nashville; author, *Is God Anti-Gay?* and *Why Does God Care Who I Sleep With?*

In an increasingly unpredictable world, which throws up phenomena from "culture wars" to "vibe shifts," Christians need more than ever to understand the deep currents at work in our culture. *The Gospel After Christendom* explains what cultural apologetics is, the various ways in which it can be pursued, and the kinds of big questions that it can address. Readers will find elucidating, encouraging, and helpful chapters from experts in a variety of areas who are continuing the legacy of Tim Keller in understanding, and speaking the gospel into, our cultural moment.

—Dr. Sarah Irving-Stonebraker, associate professor of history at Australian Catholic University and author of *Priests of History: Stewarding the Past in an Ahistoric Age*

Culture is a moving target. Thus, Christians must be deliberate, nimble, and shrewd in the practice of cultural apologetics. *The Gospel After Christendom* is a helpful resource in developing the grace and dexterity to effectively evangelize in the culture, while maintaining the courage and convictions to reject the idols of the culture.

—Justin E. Giboney, president of AND Campaign

Just like the weather, culture is changing rapidly, and Christians are quickly discovering how challenging it is to navigate the emerging cultural climate. *The Gospel After Christendom* is an excellent resource to help them chart a way forward. Drawing from a diverse group of Christian thinkers, it not only frames the key issues but also offers practical wisdom for cultural engagement. I encourage pastors and Christian leaders to pick up a copy and explore how Christianity can thoughtfully and faithfully engage in cultural apologetics.

—Stephen O. Presley, PhD, associate professor of church history, The Southern Baptist Theological Seminary

The label may be relatively new, but from the time Paul first set foot in Athens, if not before, Christians have engaged in cultural apologetics. It is perennially necessary, but especially important for the church's witness in the West today. This book helpfully covers the what, why, how, and where of cultural apologetics with material that is fresh, insightful, and eminently practical.

—James N. Anderson, Carl W. McMurray Professor of Theology and Philosophy, Reformed Theological Seminary, Charlotte

For many of us, the word *apologetics* started to leave a bad taste in our mouths, since it too often reflected Enlightenment assumptions and sensibilities while also generating a tone and attitude that seemed more combative than loving, more arrogant than thoughtful. Our apologetics must be holistic (head, hands, and heart), culturally informed, and gospel saturated. Consequently, I am especially thankful for this volume, which is both substantive and generous in content and tone. There is much here for all of us as we seek to give a reason for the hope that lies within us.

—Kelly M. Kapic, Covenant College

Cultural apologetics is not new; it retrieves a historic, holistic, and hopeful approach to Christian witness. This volume helps us reckon with the cross-pressures of our secular age, its apathy and activism, hubris and despair. These authors show us how to listen more carefully and testify more convincingly to the beauty, goodness, and truth that is found in Christ alone.

—Justin Ariel Bailey, dean of chapel and professor of theology, Dordt University

This book is a marvelous primer in an age-old practice with a catchy new name: cultural apologetics. It takes us behind the arguments and proofs often debated by those assessing the intellectual merits of Christianity and explores the more basic, instinctual, imaginative, and affective lives of those seeking goodness, truth, and beauty. It offers a witness designed not merely for the head but for the heart and hands as well—helping us address the inclinations and assumptions of our post-Christian age and reorient our loves in the way of Jesus Christ.

—Douglas A. Sweeney, Beeson Divinity School, Samford University

What an outstanding guide to the practice of cultural apologetics! *The Gospel After Christendom* equips church leaders to live as wise cultural climatologists, adapting their witness to the unchanging glories of Jesus to face the challenges of ever-changing cultural contexts. The authors are well aware of the challenges of our current moment, but they do not give in to pessimism or panic. The result is a resource that is clear and yet kind, uncompromising but still meek, concerned with current challenges and still rich with hope.

—Timothy Paul Jones, PhD, C. Edwin Gheens Professor of Christian Family Ministry and chair of apologetics, ethics, and philosophy, The Southern Baptist Theological Seminary

The Gospel After Christendom

The Gospel After Christendom

An Introduction to Cultural Apologetics

COLLIN HANSEN, SKYLER R. FLOWERS, AND IVAN MESA, EDITORS

ZONDERVAN REFLECTIVE

The Gospel After Christendom
Copyright © 2025 by The Gospel Coalition

Published by Zondervan, 3950 Sparks Drive SE, Suite 101, Grand Rapids, MI 49546, USA. Zondervan is a registered trademark of The Zondervan Corporation, L.L.C., a wholly owned subsidiary of HarperCollins Christian Publishing, Inc.

Requests for information should be addressed to customercare@harpercollins.com.

Zondervan titles may be purchased in bulk for educational, business, fundraising, or sales promotional use. For information, please email SpecialMarkets@Zondervan.com.

ISBN 978-0-310-17556-8 (audio)

Library of Congress Cataloging-in-Publication Data

Names: Hansen, Collin, 1981– editor | Flowers, Skyler R. editor | Mesa, Ivan editor
Title: The gospel after Christendom : an introduction to cultural apologetics / Collin Hansen, Skyler R. Flowers, and Ivan Mesa, editors.
Description: Grand Rapids, Michigan : Zondervan, [2025] | Includes bibliographical references and index.
Identifiers: LCCN 2025011776 (print) | LCCN 2025011777 (ebook) | ISBN 9780310175476 hardcover | ISBN 9780310175483 ebook
Subjects: LCSH: Apologetics—United States | Christianity and culture—United States | Evangelical and Reformed Church—Missions
Classification: LCC BT1103 .G665 2025 (print) | LCC BT1103 (ebook) | DDC 239--dc23/eng/20250602
LC record available at https://lccn.loc.gov/2025011776
LC ebook record available at https://lccn.loc.gov/2025011777

Unless otherwise noted, Scripture quotations are taken from the ESV® Bible (The Holy Bible, English Standard Version®). Copyright © 2001 by Crossway, a publishing ministry of Good News Publishers. Used by permission. All rights reserved.

Scripture quotations marked NIV are taken from the Holy Bible, New International Version®, NIV®. Copyright © 1973, 1978, 1984, 2011 by Biblica, Inc.® Used by permission of Zondervan. All rights reserved worldwide. www.Zondervan.com. The "NIV" and "New International Version" are trademarks registered in the United States Patent and Trademark Office by Biblica, Inc.®

Any internet addresses (websites, blogs, etc.) and telephone numbers in this book are offered as a resource. They are not intended in any way to be or imply an endorsement by Zondervan, nor does Zondervan vouch for the content of these sites and numbers for the life of this book.

All rights reserved. No part of this publication may be reproduced, stored in a retrieval system, or transmitted in any form or by any means—electronic, mechanical, photocopy, recording, or any other—except for brief quotations in printed reviews, without the prior permission of the publisher.

Without limiting the exclusive rights of any author, contributor or the publisher of this publication, any unauthorized use of this publication to train generative artificial intelligence (AI) technologies is expressly prohibited. HarperCollins also exercise their rights under Article 4(3) of the Digital Single Market Directive 2019/790 and expressly reserve this publication from the text and data mining exception.

HarperCollins Publishers, Macken House, 39/40 Mayor Street Upper, Dublin 1, D01 C9W8, Ireland (https://www.harpercollins.com)

Cover design: Brian Bobel Design
Cover image: © Ultraforma / GettyImages
Interior design: Denise Froehlich

Printed in the United States of America

25 26 27 28 29 LBC 8 7 6 5 4

For Timothy J. Keller (1950–2023),
cultural apologist par excellence
and mentor to us all

Contents

Part 3: What Questions Does Cultural Apologetics Answer?

Part 4: Where Does Cultural Apologetics Happen?

Contributors

Sam Chan (PhD, Trinity Evangelical Divinity School) is the head trainer and mentor at the EvQ school of evangelism, an initiative of the City Bible Forum. He speaks around the world on the practice of evangelism in a post-Christian culture. He shares the gospel with high schoolers, city workers, lawyers, doctors, and college students. Sam is the author of the award-winning book *Evangelism in a Skeptical World*. He blogs at EspressoTheology.com.

Joshua D. Chatraw is the Beeson Divinity School Billy Graham Chair for Evangelism and Cultural Engagement at Samford University. His recent books include *The Augustine Way*, *Surprised by Doubt*, and *Telling a Better Story*. He also serves as an inaugural fellow with the Keller Center for Cultural Apologetics and a fellow at the Center for Pastor Theologians.

James P. Eglinton (PhD, University of Edinburgh) is the Meldrum Senior Lecturer in Reformed Theology at the University of Edinburgh. He is the author of *Bavinck: A Critical Biography* and *Trinity and Organism*. He edited and translated *Herman Bavinck on Preaching and Preachers*, coedited and cotranslated *Christian Worldview*, and coedited *Neo-Calvinism and the French Revolution*. He has written for *Christianity Today*, *The Times, The Herald, The Scotsman, Nederlands Dagblad*, and the Australian Broadcasting Corporation.

Skyler R. Flowers is an associate pastor at Grace Bible Church in Oxford, Mississippi, and the associate program director at the Keller Center for Cultural Apologetics. He earned an MDiv from Reformed Theological Seminary in Orlando, Florida, and he is currently a PhD student at the University of Aberdeen. Skyler and his wife, Brianna, have two children.

Rachel Gilson serves on the leadership team of theological development and culture with Cru. She is the author of *Born Again This Way: Coming Out, Coming to Faith, and What Comes Next* and *Parenting Without Panic in an LGBT-Affirming World: Discipling Our Kids with Jesus' Truth and Love*. Rachel holds an MDiv from Gordon-Conwell Theological Seminary and is currently pursuing a PhD in public theology at Southeastern Baptist Theological Seminary.

Collin Hansen serves as vice president for content and editor in chief of The Gospel Coalition, as well as executive director of the Keller Center for Cultural Apologetics. He hosts the *Gospelbound* podcast and has written and contributed to many books, including *Timothy Keller: His Spiritual and Intellectual Formation* and *Rediscover Church: Why the Body of Christ Is Essential*. He has published with *The New York Times* and *The Washington Post* and offered commentary for CNN, Fox News, NPR, BBC, ABC News, and *PBS NewsHour*. He is an adjunct professor at Beeson Divinity School, where he also cochairs the advisory board.

Rebecca McLaughlin holds a PhD in Renaissance literature from Cambridge University and a degree in theological and pastoral studies from Oak Hill Theological College in London. She is the author of *Confronting Christianity: 12 Hard Questions for the World's Largest Religion*—named Book of the Year 2020 by *Christianity Today*—as well as *10 Questions Every Teen Should Ask (and Answer) About Christianity*, *The Secular Creed: Engaging 5 Contemporary Claims*, and *Is*

Christmas Unbelievable?Four Questions Everyone Should Ask About the World's Most Famous Story.

Ivan Mesa (PhD, Southern Baptist Theological Seminary) is editorial director of The Gospel Coalition. He's editor of *Before You Lose Your Faith* and coeditor of *Scrolling Ourselves to Death* and *Faithful Exiles*. He and his wife, Sarah, have four children, and they live in eastern Georgia.

Alan Noble (PhD, Baylor University) is associate professor of English at Oklahoma Baptist University. He has written for *The Atlantic*, Vox, BuzzFeed, The Gospel Coalition, *Christianity Today*, and *First Things*. He is also the author of *Disruptive Witness*, *You Are Not Your Own*, and *On Getting Out of Bed.*

Gavin Ortlund (PhD, Fuller Theological Seminary) serves as the president of Truth Unites, theologian-in-residence at Immanuel Nashville, and visiting professor of historical theology at Phoenix Seminary. He is the author of several books, including *Why God Makes Sense in a World That Doesn't* and *What It Means to Be Protestant.*

Derek Rishmawy (PhD, Trinity Evangelical Divinity School) is the Reformed University Fellowship (RUF) campus minister at University of California, Irvine.

Daniel Strange (PhD, University of Bristol) is director of Crosslands Forum, a center for cultural engagement, and he's in theological leadership at the London Project (City to City). He is a visiting professor at Southeastern Baptist Theological Seminary and a fellow of the Keller Center for Cultural Apologetics. Daniel is the author of *Their Rock Is Not Like Our Rock: A Theology of Religions*, *Plugged In*, and *Making Faith Magnetic*. He is a contributing editor for *Themelios* and an elder of Hope Community Church, Gateshead, UK.

N. Gray Sutanto (PhD, University of Edinburgh) is associate professor of systematic theology at Reformed Theological Seminary in Washington, DC. He is the author of *God and Knowledge* and *God and Humanity*, coauthor of *Neo-Calvinism: A Theological Introduction*, cotranslator of Herman Bavinck's *Christian Worldview*, and coeditor of *Handbook to Neo-Calvinism*. Gray is married to Indita, and they have two daughters. He is an ordained minister in the International Presbyterian Church.

Bob Thune (MA, Reformed Theological Seminary) is the founding and lead pastor of Coram Deo Church in Omaha, Nebraska. He is the author of *Gospel Eldership* and *Gospel Training for Deacons*, coauthor of *The Gospel-Centered Life* and *The Gospel-Centered Community*, and creator of *The Daily Liturgy* podcast. In addition to his work as a pastor and writer, he helps to lead a classical Christian school, coaches and trains church leaders, and serves on the council of The Gospel Coalition.

Christopher Watkin is associate professor of French and Francophone studies at Monash University, Melbourne, Australia. His books include *Difficult Atheism*, *French Philosophy Today*, and *Biblical Critical Theory: How the Bible's Unfolding Story Makes Sense of Modern Life and Culture*. Many of his talks and interviews are available on thinkingthroughthebible.com, and you can find him on X (formerly Twitter) @DrChrisWatkin.

Trevin Wax is vice president of resources and marketing at the North American Mission Board and a visiting professor at Cedarville University. A former missionary to Romania, Trevin is a regular columnist at The Gospel Coalition and has contributed to *The Washington Post*, *World*, and *Christianity Today*. He has taught courses on mission and ministry at Wheaton College and has lectured on Christianity and culture at Oxford University. He is a founding editor of the

Gospel Project, has served as publisher for the Christian Standard Bible, and is currently a fellow for the Keller Center for Cultural Apologetics. He is the author of multiple books, including *The Thrill of Orthodoxy*, *The Multi-Directional Leader*, *Rethink Your Self*, *This Is Our Time*, and *Gospel-Centered Teaching*. His podcast is *Reconstructing Faith*. Trevin and his wife, Corina, have three children.

Acknowledgments

The three of us editors have the joy of serving at The Gospel Coalition where we on a daily basis think through cultural apologetics—understanding the world we live in and strategizing ways to make the gospel of Jesus Christ clear and compelling in our secular age. Tim Keller's influence on our work at TGC is deep and abiding, as he (along with D. A. Carson) cofounded our organization twenty years ago and served as one of our biggest cheerleaders and conversation partners. Over the years, several of us had the opportunity to dialogue with Tim about the topics of this book. So it was only natural that these efforts gradually blossomed into the Keller Center for Cultural Apologetics, with its inaugural group of fellows picking up the torch in fresh and faithful ways. Since launching in 2023, the Keller Center has increased the time and other resources we can devote to this leading edge of ministry as we pray that God would make us faithful in the task of evangelism and discipleship. In many ways, this book is the fruit of Tim's passion and the areas that were top of mind and heart in the final years of his life. We dedicate this volume to him. May his tribe increase!

Introduction

We Need Cultural Climatologists

COLLIN HANSEN

Back in 2016, I asked the noted sociologist James Davison Hunter a few questions about that season's tumultuous political campaigns. Who better to answer than the scholar who popularized the phrase "culture war"?[1] His response startled me. He waved off my questions and said he doesn't forecast the weather.

He studies climatology.

The message stuck with me. We need more cultural climatologists today. We need people not just responding to the immediate events in our daily newsfeed ("the weather") but also studying and assessing the deeper-rooted values, ideologies, narratives, and patterns at work in our culture ("the climate").

At the Keller Center for Cultural Apologetics, we don't necessarily think cultural apologetics is the only—or even always the best—way to defend the Christian faith. But we do think the climate is ripe for cultural apologetics. This practice connects us to vital

1. James Davison Hunter, *Culture Wars: The Struggle to Control the Family, Art, Education, Law, and Politics in America* (New York: Basic, 1991).

sources of biblical, theological, and historical wisdom so we can share and apply the gospel in compelling ways for our secular age.

Indeed, we're living amid the largest religious transformation in American history. Some forty million Americans have left the church in the last twenty-five to thirty years.[2] Many other Western countries have already seen similar declines. But that's not the only challenge. Since the decline and fall of Christendom, as church attendance cratered across many Western nations in the twentieth century, believers in Western countries now face a strange mixture of apathy and antagonism toward the gospel. Many of our neighbors view Christianity as yesterday's news but also as the source of today's problems.

This is a new challenge. A big challenge. And many church leaders have no idea what to do. We hope this book will help.

It's All Cultural

For many, apologetics is associated with arguments over rational, philosophical proofs. It's a matter of the head instead of the heart, a debate over facts instead of feelings.

But no matter what kind of apologetics you practice, you're arguing according to a certain set of rules, in a particular language, attuned to what you expect to resonate in your time and place. In other words, it's always cultural, never purely timeless.[3] And it's never purely rational.

We need to recover apologetics as a matter of the heart and hands as well as the head. We need to recover apologetics as a project for the whole church and not just for those who enjoy arguing. Cultural apologetics isn't a new academic discipline. It's a means to reconnect

2. Jim Davis and Michael Graham, with Ryan P. Burge, *The Great Dechurching: Who's Leaving, Why Are They Going, and What Will It Take to Bring Them Back?* (Grand Rapids: Zondervan Reflective, 2023).
3. Mark Allen and Joshua D. Chatraw, *The Augustine Way: Retrieving a Vision for the Church's Apologetic Witness* (Grand Rapids: Baker Academic, 2023).

the church to the best biblical and historical resources for presenting and defending the faith "once for all delivered to the saints" (Jude 3).

In the Gospels, we see Jesus commonly deploy illustrations from everyday life that connect with his neighbors in an agricultural society. In the book of Acts, Peter's sermon at Pentecost and Paul's sermon on Mars Hill convey the same gospel message but strike different notes based on their respective hearers: the Jewish diaspora and Greek philosophers (Acts 2:14–41; 17:16–34). Justin Martyr's *First Apology* in the second century and Augustine's *City of God* in the fifth century speak timeless truth in timely ways for dramatically different moments in the history of the Roman Empire.[4]

From these biblical and historical examples, you can see there's nothing new about cultural apologetics. No matter your strategy, you can't avoid culture, because culture itself is another way to describe what we mean by religion. Everybody worships—someone or something. Missiologist Lesslie Newbigin argued that culture is really just another way we describe religion, how we pursue meaning and understanding from life.[5]

Religion isn't downstream from culture. Culture is downstream from religion, the inevitable human pursuit of meaning and eternity. And we see that pursuit everywhere we turn, from dense academic texts down to catchy television jingles. Everything from hip-hop music to arthouse films conveys our society's deepest longings. Watch a sporting event, especially in person, and you'll learn a culture's hopes and fears.

In this book, we provide tools to develop your climatology skills. Rooted in the gospel, we want to help amateur and experienced apologists correct and connect to their cultures so they can better help non-Christians see their sin and seek the Savior.

4. Justin Martyr, *The First and Second Apologies*, trans. Leslie William Barnard (Mahwah, NJ: Newman, 1997); Augustine, *The City of God*, trans. Marcus Dods (New York City: Modern Library, 1994).
5. Lesslie Newbigin, *Foolishness to the Greeks: The Gospel and Western Culture* (Grand Rapids: Eerdmans, 1986).

Bridge of Hope

Apologetics can never be purely rational because the head never reasons alone. Culture shapes which desires we indulge and which we reject. In the Augustinian tradition, cultural apologists recognize desire as a key motivator for faith.

Social psychologist Jonathan Haidt has described the relationship between intuition and reason as an elephant and its rider. Reason may steer, but intuition will only move when motivated. What the heart wants, the head will rationalize. Our intuitions follow our aspirations: What kind of person do I want to be? Or, to ask the same question another way, who's my tribe? We might imagine ourselves as independent, rational actors who weigh arguments with careful consideration of objective truth. More often, we're activated by tribal instincts that filter which beliefs we're willing to entertain—let alone which beliefs we would allow to transform our lives. Until we want to change, until we can envision ourselves in a new community, we're not likely to lower our rational defenses.[6]

Cultural apologetics, then, helps non-Christians want the gospel to be true even before they may fully understand this good news. We offer the beauty of the lordship of Christ as opposed to the ugliness of the lordship of the principalities and powers (Eph. 6:12).

Against pervasive cultural nihilism across the West, we offer hope. In Christ, we find fulfillment to our desires for beauty, justice, peace, truth, and goodness.[7] Most people will find that hope in the context of church community, where they see the effects of the gospel in changed lives.[8] The church can provide an alternative climate, a life-giving atmosphere that challenges the dark clouds of the surrounding cultural weather system. Christians themselves are the

6. Jonathan Haidt, *The Righteous Mind: Why Good People Are Divided by Politics and Religion* (New York: Vintage, 2012).
7. Ted Turnau, *Popologetics: Popular Culture in Christian Perspective* (Phillipsburg, NJ: P&R, 2012).
8. Lesslie Newbigin, *The Gospel in a Pluralist Society* (Grand Rapids: Eerdmans, 1989); Alan Kreider, *The Patient Ferment of the Early Church* (Grand Rapids: Baker, 2016).

best bridge between hope and non-Christians. The world sees Jesus in how the body of Christ lives together with grace, in truth, for love. Thus, cultural apologetics seeks spiritual and moral renewal in the church as testimony to the gospel's transforming power.

Paul Gould defines cultural apologetics as the "work of establishing the Christian voice, conscience, and imagination within a culture so that Christianity is seen as true and satisfying."[9] In this noisy culture, with seemingly infinite voices competing for attention, the church captures the imagination of non-Christians when we love them and each other. This is what Jesus prayed in John 17:23—the world will know the Father sent him when we are one.

Of course, no one will conclude just from watching our life together that Jesus is the Son of God, that he died and rose for sinners, and that he's coming again soon to renew the heavens and the earth. We must tell them this good news, warn them to repent of their sin, and call them to believe. When they can see the gospel's effects in us, non-Christians can better recognize this news as good. Surely they will see us fall short; they will see us fail; they will see us sin. We don't offer them perfection. We point them to the same blood of Christ that washed away our sin. Those who know they have been forgiven are full of love for fellow sinners (Luke 7:47).

Compelling Community

Love, however, is not the most common perception of the church today by outsiders. Shortly before the 2016 presidential election, I met with a group of Christian students at Cornell University. They had invited me to Ithaca to speak on the history of the Religious Right—not exactly a powerful force on their Ivy League campus. Still, the topic was relevant because of how Christians in far-flung corners of the United States could affect their reputation and mission in upstate New York.

9. Paul M. Gould, *Cultural Apologetics: Renewing the Christian Voice, Conscience, and Imagination in a Disenchanted World* (Grand Rapids: Zondervan, 2019), 21.

I asked these students what their classmates associate first with Christianity. I couldn't believe their answer. Since then I've repeated the question with audiences around the country. And every time I hear the same thing.

Westboro Baptist Church.

So, I said with some bemusement, let me get this straight: When students at one of the nation's most prestigious universities consider the world's largest religion, they think about an overgrown family cult in Topeka, Kansas. How can this be?

No matter how persuasive our cultural apologetics may be, we shouldn't always expect a positive response. Indeed, Jesus promised us tribulation (John 16:33). Peter warned us that honorable conduct wouldn't guarantee favor from non-Christians (1 Pet. 2:12). At the same time, Paul emphasized that negative perceptions of the church can stem from immoral behavior in the church (1 Cor. 5:1; Rom. 2:1). Sometimes we get what we deserve.

I attribute some of the church's perception problems to a superficial understanding of culture—too much weather, not enough climate. Weather often gravitates toward focusing on what's wrong with others. Climate focuses on the conditions that affect everyone, inside and outside the church. Maybe we don't see more evangelistic fruit because the church doesn't look much different from the world. What is compelling about our community?[10] Instead of living for Christ, we're often conforming to the world. Even in many evangelical churches, the gospel has become an accessory to middle-class mores. We might vote a certain way to "save the culture," meaning, to oppose the evil of our political opponents. But what about our own cultural captivity to consumerism or convenience or comfort? How does the church stand out by offering fear and loathing in a world already full of it?

Consider the difference with a community that shows love

10. Mark Dever and Jamie Dunlop, *The Compelling Community: Where God's Power Makes a Church Attractive* (Wheaton, IL: Crossway, 2015).

even to outsiders, even to enemies (Matt. 5:44). Consider a community that counts others more important than themselves (Phil. 2:3). Consider a community that realizes we only find life when we lose it (Matt. 10:38–39). The culture of that community commands attention even from a skeptical world. That community will help non-Christians see the transforming power and hope of the gospel. That community will shock the world by admitting its own flaws and mistakes instead of covering them up.

One Storm to Another

It's easy to forecast the weather as cloudy with a 100 percent chance of culture war. But climatology tells us we're in the eye of the civilizational hurricane. We've passed through one destructive storm. Now, we enter another. For hundreds of years, Christian values supplied the beloved and fiercely defended foundation of Western civilization—tolerance, minority rights, equal justice, and much more. But Christianity has been forgotten (at best) or blamed (at worst) in what philosopher Charles Taylor describes as the "subtraction story" of secularism—we could have everything we want if we just subtracted Christianity.[11]

Secularism, however, hasn't delivered a stable new foundation for the West. The so-called Enlightenment, too, has fallen despite attempts to ground universal values without help from religion.[12] Cultural apologetics helps us observe how secularism remains a spiritual project searching for a common good. Sociologist Christian Smith writes,

> To make everything new, to leave behind the past, to be unbound by any tradition, to enjoy maximum choice, to be free from any

11. Charles Taylor, *A Secular Age* (Cambridge: Belknap, 2007).
12. Jonathan Rauch, *The Constitution of Knowledge: A Defense of Truth* (Washington, DC: Brookings Institution, 2021).

> constraint, to be able to buy whatever one can afford, to live however one desires—that is the guiding vision of modernity's spiritual project. It is spiritual (not merely ideological or cultural) because it names what is sacrosanct, an ultimate concern, a vision for what is most worthy in a sense that transcends any individual life. It is spiritual because it speaks to people's deepest personal subjectivities, their most transcendent vision of goodness, their definition of ultimate fulfillment. It is spiritual because as a deep cultural structure it occupies a position in the modern West homologous with salvation in God that was prized in the premodern Christendom that modernity broke apart. And it is spiritual because, by being sacred, it is worth protecting, defending, policing, fighting for, perhaps dying for, even killing for.[13]

In every way, our secular age remains very religious (Acts 17:22). No less than the chair of the department of human evolutionary biology at Harvard University argues that Christianity has shaped our very psychology in the West. Joseph Henrich says Christian values, applied over centuries, made us WEIRD: Western, educated, industrialized, rich, and democratic.[14] But we can't see this Christian influence on our culture because secularism tried to recast these religious values as universal truths. So explains the award-winning historian and podcast host Tom Holland. He told me, "The genius of the modern West in recent centuries has been that it has been able to export its profoundly Christian values, concepts like human rights, the notion of consent—all these things are deeply rooted in the seedbed of Christian history and Christian theology."[15] A key example is

13. Christian Smith, *To Flourish or Destruct: A Personalist Account of Human Goods, Motivations, Failure, and Evil* (Chicago: University of Chicago Press, 2015), 269–70.
14. Joseph Henrich, *The WEIRDest People in the World: How the West Became Psychologically Peculiar and Particularly Prosperous* (New York: Farrar, Straus and Giroux, 2020).
15. Tom Holland, interview with Collin Hansen, *Gospelbound*, podcast audio, March 10, 2020, https://www.thegospelcoalition.org/podcasts/gospelbound/the-revolution-the-west-wishes-it-could-forget/.

the 1948 *Universal Declaration of Human Rights*, which owes much to Christian assumptions but doesn't mention God.

Indeed, Christianity is a revolution that remade the world. Holland asks, "How was it that a cult inspired by the execution of an obscure criminal in a long-vanished empire came to exercise such a transformative and enduring influence on the world?"[16] In Holland's narrative, the church has become a victim of its own success. Christianity is so pervasive that Western culture doesn't even know it's there. When Christians in Hong Kong protest for democracy, or when Christians in India fight caste-based racism, they're seen as acting for universal progress and not merely a Christian worldview. "If they cast them as Christian values," Holland told me, "then they'd come to seem more culturally contingent to people in India or wherever. If you say, well no, they're universal, then you can export them."[17]

We need cultural apologetics, then, to show that what we cherish about our culture depends on Christianity. As we're learning today, when you lose Christianity, you also lose Enlightenment. Dark is the second wall of the hurricane we're entering. We need apologists fired with the love of Christ who will light the lamps that have gone out across the West. We need in our day what Augustine did with *City of God* as the Eternal City and its empire crumbled in the fifth century.

At the Keller Center, and in this book, we seek to support such efforts. Even now you can see flickers of hope, such as Christopher Watkin's *Biblical Critical Theory*,[18] Rebecca McLaughlin's *The Secular Creed*,[19] and Andrew Wilson's *Remaking the World*.[20] Much more work remains to be done, as you'll see in the ensuing chapters.

16. Tom Holland, *Dominion: How the Christian Revolution Remade the World* (New York: Basic, 2019), 12.
17. Tom Holland, interview with Collin Hansen, *Gospelbound*.
18. Christopher Watkin, *Biblical Critical Theory: How the Bible's Unfolding Story Makes Sense of Modern Life and Culture* (Grand Rapids: Zondervan Academic, 2022).
19. Rebecca McLaughlin, *The Secular Creed: Engaging Five Contemporary Claims* (Austin: The Gospel Coalition, 2021).
20. Andrew Wilson, *Remaking the World: How 1776 Created the Post-Christian West* (Wheaton, IL: Crossway, 2023).

We hope this book will inspire cultural apologists in local churches, in their neighborhoods, in their classrooms, and in their workplaces. The best cultural apologists know the names of their neighbors. Those neighbors, living quietly amid anxieties they cannot name, need to know the thundering darkness of our current weather doesn't have the last word. Dawn will break; God's kingdom is just over the horizon. They need to know a happy ending is coming—when they turn from sin and trust in Christ.

From Thick to Thin

This book aims to help you discover theological, pastoral, and practical resources that define and shape cultural apologetics. Along with editors Skyler Flowers and Ivan Mesa, I have convened leading scholars and practitioners who serve as fellows at the Keller Center for Cultural Apologetics. We will seek to define cultural apologetics, explain its biblical and historical grounding, and demonstrate how it is important for the church today.

Our fellows don't agree on everything you will read in this volume. They emphasize complementary aspects of cultural apologetics and sometimes differ in the details of a formal definition for this discipline. Such disagreement makes for lively annual retreats in New York! But this diversity of viewpoints, still united in the gospel, has enriched our gathering. In their differences, with complementary gifts and vocations, our fellows push, stretch, and reinforce one another spiritually and intellectually. Such was Tim Keller's vision for the center from its beginning, shortly before his death in 2023. "I'm so grateful for the ministry of the Keller Center," he wrote us. "A major part of what I've tried to accomplish in recent years is to encourage younger writers, scholars, and ministers who are doing exactly what the church in the United States needs to do in order to reach people for Christ. There are many such men and women out there, and they need lots of support. I'm delighted that the Keller

Center will carry this work on for me." This center, and its fellows, share Keller's desire above all else that many would come to know Jesus Christ as he is revealed and offered in the gospel.

Part 1 lays the conceptual foundation of our approach to cultural apologetics. Trevin Wax begins by considering the twenty-first-century Western cultural context and offers cultural apologetics as a way that the church might reach the West again (chapter 1). Christopher Watkin follows by demonstrating that cultural apologetics isn't a modern invention but a methodology displayed in the pages of Scripture itself (chapter 2). Joshua D. Chatraw continues this line of thinking through church history, offering numerous historical examples—notably Augustine—who have shaped Christianity's cultural apologetic (chapter 3).

Part 2 turns to the task of cultural apologetics. Alan Noble opens with our posture, which is neither accommodation nor aggression (chapter 4). Daniel Strange helps us enter the narratives of a culture, discover their idolatrous co-opting of the Christian story, and demonstrate how the Christian story offers a glorious fulfillment of these hopes and desires (chapter 5). Gray Sutanto builds a holistic theological anthropology that attends to how humans know God and suppress that knowledge in sin (chapter 6). Gavin Ortlund concludes the section by showing how to expose unbelief as not merely untrue but also unlivable and how the gospel answers this despair (chapter 7).

Part 3 drills down into various topics cultural apologists will encounter, namely, the pursuit of truth, goodness, and beauty. Against many skeptics and detractors, Christianity offers moral goodness in a vision for flourishing, according to Rebecca McLaughlin (chapter 8). Rachel Gilson presents a picture of Christianity's inherent beauty—compelling just as it is comprehensible and commendable (chapter 9). Derek Rishmawy concludes with a reminder that the Christian story is the grounding reality for all of life (chapter 10).

Finally, part 4 visits the places where cultural apologetics can be deployed. Beginning with its proper home, Bob Thune turns our attention to the church, institutionally and organically, as it proclaims and embodies the gospel (chapter 11). James Eglinton advances the church's work by considering how Christians might create spaces for engaging non-Christians to safely learn and explore Jesus's claims (chapter 12). To conclude our volume, Sam Chan draws on the resources of preceding chapters to demonstrate for Christians how cultural apologetics can enrich their everyday conversations over cultural texts (chapter 13).

In this book you'll see that cultural apologetics ranges between academic discourse and everyday experiences. From thick books to thin veneers of social graces, cultural apologetics helps Christians live what they believe and proclaim: the gospel that is true for all and good for individuals in unique ways.

Look past the ten-day forecast. Study the climate. Through every weather pattern, the Word of the Lord stands forever (Isa. 40:8). On the other side of this cultural hurricane, you'll find the peace and calm of a kingdom that will never end.

PART 1

What Is Cultural Apologetics?

1

A Tool for Evangelism

TREVIN WAX

In his 1896 lecture "The Will to Believe," American philosopher William James (1842–1910) described religious beliefs as either "live" or "dead" wires. A live hypothesis is a real possibility for someone. For example, James said, if he were to ask you to believe in the Mahdi (someone claiming to be the messianic figure in Islam who is to appear at the End Times to rid the world of evil and injustice), you'd probably not even know what was being asked. There's no "electric connection with your nature." No spark of credibility at all. It's a *dead wire* for you. But if he were to ask an Arab (even if not one of the Mahdi's followers), the possibility would be live. "Deadness and liveness in a hypothesis are not intrinsic properties," James said, "but relations to the individual thinker."[1]

The possibility of a religious belief is either a live or dead wire.

1. William James, *The Will to Believe, and Other Essays in Popular Philosophy* (Auckland, New Zealand: Floating, 2010), 14–15.

"A living option is one in which both hypotheses are live ones." For many in James's time, the choice between being a Muslim or a theosophist was basically a "dead option," but the choice between being "an agnostic or a Christian" was alive. (And many of his contemporaries opted for agnosticism over traditional Christianity.)

Today we're witnessing both a rise in secularism and a corresponding decline in the percentage of people who belong to religious organizations or claim religious faith. Around forty million Americans have left the church in the last twenty-five years.[2] Other countries have seen similar declines. Such a massive shift in religious demographics cannot help but alter a society's underlying beliefs, desires, and hopes. There was a time when the decision *not* to adhere to a religious tradition was rare and atheism implausible. Today, the plausibility structures have shifted to the point where it's more unusual in some places to believe in God or to attend church than to not.

For centuries in the West, much of human life was understood within the conceptual framework of a society influenced by Christianity. Belief in an unseen realm, or the assumption of heaven or hell after death, or the reality of human sin and the need for divine salvation—these were so widespread as marks of "common-sense thinking" that the evangelistic task was relatively straightforward: *Show that Jesus is the One who overcomes the powers of evil and brings deliverance from sin. Show that Jesus is the only Way to eternal life because he took on himself the punishment for our sin. Show that we're sinners in need of a Savior, and Jesus is the Son of God who meets us in our need and accomplishes our redemption.* With the fading of a Christian framework in society, these cultural touchpoints can no longer be assumed. An evangelist's work becomes more complex. We often have to start further back—whether we're talking about God's existence, distinguishing between cultural conceptions of sin and what the Bible says about human depravity, or making a case for the goodness and beauty of the church.

2. Davis and Graham, with Burge, *The Great Dechurching.*

In a world where shared cultural assumptions have been lost, what does it mean to call someone to follow Jesus? In a world where religion is personalized and privatized, often relegated to the realm of chosen values and not public truth, many people will assume when we share the gospel that we're merely recommending a new type of religious experience, something to help achieve inner peace or cope with the vicissitudes of our modern world. And if Christianity continues to decline, it's possible at some point that calling someone to follow Jesus will make about as much sense as asking the average American in 1896 if they'll follow the Mahdi. If secularism slowly remakes Christianity into a less plausible option, a "dead wire" for most people, how should we respond?

Cultural apologetics is one way of addressing these concerns, a way both new and old of preparing the soil for the gospel seed. It's old because the approach has an ancient pedigree, something we can trace back through the centuries of church history. It's new because we've often overlooked this tool in recent decades, as we've been slow to realize many of the cultural touchpoints we once assumed no longer exist, and we've sometimes opted for a one-size-fits-all approach to making a case for the gospel. It's an old tool in the toolkit, but it needs to be dusted off and repurposed for today's world.

Cultural Apologetics as a Tool

This approach begins with a particular posture toward the culture. The missionary theologian Lesslie Newbigin (1909–98) urged Christians toward a missionary encounter between the gospel and whatever culture we are trying to reach.[3] We want to present Christianity in a way that is comprehensible, commendable, and

3. See Lesslie Newbigin, *The Gospel in a Pluralist Society* (Grand Rapids: Eerdmans, 1989); Newbigin, *Foolishness to the Greeks: The Gospel and Western Culture* (Grand Rapids: Eerdmans, 1988); Michael W. Goheen, *The Church and Its Vocation: Lesslie Newbigin's Missionary Ecclesiology* (Grand Rapids: Baker Academic, 2018).

compelling in our context. Likewise, we don't want to appeal only to the mind but also to the heart and to the imagination as we cultivate the soil and pray for its receptivity to the seed.

In this light, cultural apologetics is a form of preevangelism. It requires us to listen carefully and then enter the story of a culture so we can "renarrate" someone's outlook on the world. We shine the light of the gospel in a way that affirms their God-given deepest longings and aspirations while exposing the misdirection that leads to lies, half-truths, and unhappiness. Cultural apologetics does this twofold work: showing how the gospel fulfills the deepest longings of the people in a society *and* exposing the lies people in that society believe. Often the longings and lies are connected. It's the longing for transcendence, for a relationship with God, when misdirected, that leads us to believe lies and to fall for falsehoods.[4]

Cultural apologetics is about discovering what makes people in a culture "tick." *Why do they believe what they believe? What is plausible in this society? What is their view of the good life?* We can discern these sensibilities in films; in television series; in books, songs, musicals, and even YouTube tutorials; and especially in one-on-one conversations. This manner of apologetics examines the culture and then looks for ways to bring the truth of the gospel to bear into a missionary encounter with that culture.

If traditional apologetics is about making arguments to defend Christian truth, *cultural* apologetics is about making arguments that showcase Christianity's beauty and goodness, using cultural touchpoints as an opportunity for gospel witness. It's a precursor to evangelism. It sets the stage so the gospel's beauty can be accentuated.

In what follows, I offer four reasons why cultural apologetics should no longer be a neglected tool but a necessary way of engaging people in a secularizing world.

4. This is the construct of my book *This Is Our Time: Everyday Myths in Light of the Gospel* (Nashville: B&H, 2017).

1. Because We Want to Respond Wisely to New Social and Cultural Narratives

Returning to William James's analogy of dead and live wires, we may wonder, *Is Christianity—traditional Christianity and its creeds and confessions and congregations and cathedrals—a plausible option for radically secular, never-churched people? Is it a live wire, a possibility for most people? Or is it increasingly a dead wire?*

Asking this question gets to the root of anxiety among Christians today. The reason many Christians worry about Christendom's decline and the loss of traditional moral values is that it seems to make evangelism and discipleship more challenging. Likewise, the loss of cultural Christianity is met by the rise of new social and cultural narratives—different visions of the good life and how we find fulfillment.

Expressive Individualism

One of the dominant visions of life today can be summed up by the term *expressive individualism*, an outlook described in *Habits of the Heart* by Robert Bellah and several other American sociologists. Bellah defines it this way: "Expressive individualism holds that each person has a unique core and feeling of intuition that should unfold or be expressed if individuality is to be realized."[5] In other words, every person is unique, and the way we come into our own as human beings, the way we fully realize our humanity, is when that feeling of what we are inside, that spark of uniqueness, can unfold publicly.

There's another way of describing expressive individualism, which comes from the philosopher Charles Taylor's work in *The Malaise of Modernity* and *A Secular Age*.[6] He says we live in the "age

5. Robert N. Bellah et al., *Habits of the Heart: Individualism and Commitment in American Life*, new ed. (Berkeley: University of California Press, 2007), 334.
6. Charles Taylor, *The Malaise of Modernity* (Toronto: House of Anansi, 1991); later published as *The Ethics of Authenticity* (Cambridge, MA: Harvard University Press, 1992); Charles Taylor, *A Secular Age* (Cambridge, MA: Belknap, 2007).

of authenticity." Many of us Christians react positively to the word *authenticity* because we tend to pit it against *hypocrisy* (and Jesus was right to chastise hypocrites!), but this isn't the way Taylor uses the word. The opposite of *authenticity* in Taylor's telling isn't *hypocrisy* but *conformity*. To be authentic means you refuse to *conform* your life to any vision that comes from outside yourself. Here's Taylor's definition:

> The understanding of life which emerges with the Romantic expressivism of the late-eighteenth century, that each one of us has his/her own way of realizing our humanity, and that it is important to find and live out one's own, as against surrendering to conformity with a model imposed on us from outside, by society, or the previous generation, or religious or political authority.[7]

In other words, in the age of authenticity, the dominant questions are these: *How can I find my true self and express my inner essence to the world? How can I make sure the presumptions of my family, my society, my religion—all these cultural expressions—don't get in the way of me being me?*

These definitions help us understand what is meant by expressive individualism, but most of the people we talk to every day have never heard these academic terms. They're more likely to capture the ethos in slogans like "You be you," "Be true to yourself," "Follow your heart," or "Be yourself." These sayings, in one way or another, capture the essence of expressive individualism.[8] Countless self-help books reinforce this idea.

7. Taylor, *Secular Age*, 475.
8. Several recent books trace the development and influence of expressive individualism. See Trevin Wax, *Rethink Your Self: The Power of Looking Up Before Looking In* (Nashville: B&H, 2020); Carl Trueman, *The Rise and Triumph of the Modern Self: Cultural Amnesia, Expressive Individualism, and the Road to Sexual Revolution* (Wheaton, IL: Crossway, 2020); Graham Tomlin, *Why Being Yourself Is a Bad Idea: And Other Countercultural Notions* (London: SPCK, 2020).

Other Cultural Narratives

Expressive individualism is just one example of a cultural narrative that has risen in recent decades. We could point to various other outlooks on life.

Naturalism. Some see the world in purely naturalistic terms, adopting either a perspective that is atheistic and possibly hostile to religious faith or a secular mindset that, while open to some type of religious experience, interprets everything within an immanent frame, ruling out the truly transcendent.[9]

Freedom. In the United States, the value we place on freedom and the right to pursue happiness has shifted from a holistic, positive sense of becoming free *for* something (free to achieve a particular hard-won vision for success in life) to a negative sense of primarily breaking free *from* something (usually, the constraints imposed on us from close relationships, religious groups, family expectations, and so on).[10]

Identity Politics. Another social narrative that gives meaning to people in society today is seen by the upsurge in identity politics. Within an immanent frame of reference, there is no transcendent community or transcendent meaning. Thus, when someone identifies with a "tribe" and engages in identity politics, they seek to become part of a "chosen people" who are on a mission bigger than themselves, a cause that endows meaning and significance to their life. Anyone, any tribe, who opposes their mission, is opposing them personally and obstructing their pathway to finding (or making) meaning and significance.[11]

Intuitional Religions. The agnostic-versus-Christian hypothesis that William James saw as a live wire for educated people in 1896

9. Phil Zuckerman, *Living the Secular Life: New Answers to Old Questions* (New York: Penguin, 2014).
10. See Timothy Keller, *How to Reach the West Again: Six Essential Elements of a Missionary Encounter* (New York: Redeemer City to City, 2020), 39.
11. See Mary Eberstadt, *Primal Screams: How the Sexual Revolution Created Identity Politics* (West Conshohocken, PA: Templeton, 2021).

has been replaced by what Charles Taylor describes as the "nova effect"—an explosion of different options for belief and meaning in a secular age. It's not just *this* position or *that*; it's *this* choice among *that*, and *that*, and *that*, and *that*—myriad beliefs and practices, many "remixed" in some way, as pointed out by Tara Isabella Burton, who has also chronicled the shift from "institutional" religion to "intuitional" faiths.[12] It's no surprise, then, that pastors and church leaders today feel as if they must answer not only the question of "Why Christianity?" but also of "Why not whatever?"

Jesus Is Better

If we're to be good missionaries, we cannot ignore a changing cultural context. Perhaps we've gotten accustomed to relying on aspects of cultural Christianity or Christendom in the past to smooth the way for gospel presentation. We can no longer do so. In our world today, we shouldn't assume biblical literacy. We shouldn't assume a favorable atmosphere for the gospel. We shouldn't assume the plausibility of Christianity's moral vision. We shouldn't assume that the methods we've used in the past will continue to bear fruit the same way in the future. Missionaries must adapt to conditions on the ground, and so should we.

Cultural apologetics is one way of adapting our mentality and our methods to these new conditions, helping us make a holistic case for Christianity. Our response to these cultural narratives will not be to merely point out the flaws and failures in what our neighbors believe but also to show them why these outlooks on life are ultimately unsatisfying and why only Jesus brings salvation, both for this life and the next.

12. Tara Isabella Burton, *Strange Rites: New Religions for a Godless World* (New York: PublicAffairs, 2020).

2. Because Caring for Your Neighbor Implies Curiosity About the Neighborhood

Another reason why the discipline of cultural apologetics matters today? Because culture matters. There is no such thing as a non-contextualized gospel presentation. When we proclaim the gospel, we are always presenting a divine and powerful message in cultural terms. As we see in 1 Corinthians 1, the message will be a stumbling block to some (Paul preaching the message to Jews) and will sound like foolishness to others (Paul preaching the message to Greeks).

Depending on the cultural context, some aspects of Christian teaching resonate with people and others sound foolish. Not long ago, I had a conversation with a church planter in Germany whose ministry is directed to both highly secular people and immigrants from the Middle East. Sometimes, during just one day of conversations, he'll witness the same aspect of Christianity acting as a stumbling block for different reasons. The Christian view that any sex outside of marriage is sin is an obstacle for a secular German, yet for the immigrant Muslim, Christian compassion for all kinds of sexual sinners is the obstacle. In the first conversation, the pastor must explain why Christian teaching on sexuality is good and not hateful toward those who identify as LGBT. In the second conversation, the pastor must turn around and explain why Christian teaching on human sin and God's love is good and why God's mercy toward us rules out any sense of superiority or hatred toward other sexual sinners.

As more and more cultures collide in the West, we will not be able to fall back on the same apologetic method for Christianity as if all or most people are the same. One way we learn to love our neighbors effectively is to seek to understand them—what they hope for themselves and loved ones, what they think about the world, and what they want the world to be. To care about your neighbor means you'll give some attention to the neighborhood—the norms, the values, the presuppositions, the culture of the world we live in.

Cultural apologetics means we give attention to the culture not because we want to be "cool" or "relevant" or make the gospel palatable to every society. We care about culture because culture is part of human life. We can't really love our neighbors (real people in real places) if we don't care about the cultural influences and artifacts that affect "real people" or distinguish one "real place" from another. We can't love our neighbor without having some idea of our neighborhood. And cultural apologetics helps us understand the world around us so we can share the gospel in comprehensive and compelling ways.

3. Because We Address the Whole Person—the Imagination Alongside the Intellect

Jesus is the only way to God, but there are many ways to Jesus. As we call people to faith in Christ, we must be attentive to multiple realities and ways of engaging the heart. C. S. Lewis (1898–1963) was one of the last century's foremost Christian apologists, and he relied on more than one tool in the toolkit when making a case for Christianity. We encounter not only his reasoned and rational defenses for Christian truth claims but also his imaginative retellings of Christianity's story. Lewis referred to "stealing past watchful dragons" to describe how stories, particularly fantasy, can bypass the defenses of our intellect and skepticism.[13] By engaging readers' imaginations, these stories convey deeper truths and moral lessons without triggering the resistance that might arise if presented more directly.

Ken Myers, longtime host of the acclaimed *Mars Hill Audio Journal*, distinguishes traditional from cultural apologetics. "Traditional apologetics is concerned with making arguments to

13. C. S. Lewis, "Sometimes Fairy Stories May Say Best What's to Be Said," *New York Times Book Review*, November 18, 1956, 3, https://www.nytimes.com/1956/11/18/archives/sometimes-fairy-stories-may-say-best-whats-to-be-said.html.

defend Christian truth claims," he says, "and has often addressed challenges to Christian belief coming from philosophical and other more intellectual sources."[14] In contrast, cultural apologetics refers to "systematic efforts to advance the plausibility of Christian claims in light of the messages communicated through dominant cultural institutions, including films, popular music, literature, art, and the mass media." By defining cultural apologetics in this way, Myers emphasizes the role of imagination and the need for deeper understanding of influential cultural artifacts. He goes on: "So while traditional apologists would critique the challenges to the Christian faith advanced in the writings of certain philosophers, cultural apologists might look instead at the sound bite philosophies embedded in the lyrics of popular songs, the plots of popular movies, or even the slogans in advertising."

There are many roads to Jesus. For some, the journey will begin with an exploration of Christianity's truth claims. For others, it will begin with a sense of dissatisfaction and curiosity, as someone is drawn to the beauty of Christianity in the world. Some might find the church's communal life warm and inviting, what Lesslie Newbigin called the "hermeneutic of the gospel," where the gospel is put on display. More than a few will look to Jesus when life goes crazy in periods of sorrow and suffering. Still others may find their imaginations ignited by the epic stories in our world that showcase the beauty of the story of redemption, all the echoes that find their resonance in the gospel's symphony. Cultural apologetics is one way of recognizing that we bring the whole gospel to the whole human person. We cannot argue someone into the faith, as if conversion were merely the rational winning of a debate. We woo people into the faith, as we rely on the Spirit to showcase Jesus's beauty in ways that appeal to all aspects of our being.

14. Ken Myers, as quoted in Paul M. Gould, *Cultural Apologetics: Renewing the Christian Voice, Conscience, and Imagination in a Disenchanted World* (Grand Rapids: Zondervan Academic, 2019), 20. The quotes in this paragraph are taken from the same source.

4. Because the Goodness and Beauty of Jesus Are Worthy of Display

Make no mistake, the gospel is good, and Jesus is beautiful. Cultural apologists want to do justice to that beauty, to answer the question of not only why Christianity is true but why it is *good*. The French philosopher Blaise Pascal (1623–62) laid out a path for cultural apologetics several centuries ago: "Men despise religion, they hate it and are afraid it might be true. To cure that we have to begin by showing that religion is not contrary to reason. That it is worthy of veneration and should be given respect. Next it should be made lovable, should make the good wish it were true. Then show that it is indeed true."[15]

What we see here is a beautiful intersection of truth, goodness, and beauty (more on this in later chapters). Traditional apologetics helps to clear away the obstacles, to show that Christianity isn't contrary to reason but is worthy of respect. Cultural apologetics goes a step further, demonstrating the beauty of the gospel, presenting it in such a way that the person with a heart stirred by the Spirit will wish it were true. "Show it to be lovable," Pascal says. Don't just present proofs and rational arguments, important as they may be. Highlight the beauty.

One way we highlight the beauty is by remembering the church's centrality. Don't underestimate the power of relationships. The church is where Easter comes alive. A renewed fellowship of people who follow Jesus together is indispensable in the conversation about Christianity's plausibility. Charles Taylor points out the power of relationships in a world with so many religious options:

> This kind of multiplicity of faiths has little effect as long as it is neutralized by the sense that being like them is not really an option for me. As long as the alternative is strange and other,

15. Blaise Pascal, *Pensées and Other Writings: A New Translation*, trans. Honor Levi (Oxford: Oxford University Press, 1995), 12.

> perhaps despised, but perhaps just too different, too weird, too incomprehensible, so that becoming that isn't really conceivable for me, so long will their differences not undermine my embedding in my own faith.

Unless something happens that suddenly makes another person's faith option seem viable. And that happens usually through relationship. He goes on:

> This changes when through increased contact, interchange, even perhaps inter-marriage, the other becomes more and more like me, in everything else but faith. . . . Then the issue posed by the difference becomes more insistent: why my way, and not hers? There is no other difference left to make the shift preposterous or unimaginable.[16]

Rodney Stark made a similar point about early Christianity. Conversion is more likely when "people have or develop stronger attachments to members of the group than they have to nonmembers."[17] This is still true. Both personal evangelism and corporate fellowship are vital if we're to *show* the world that following Christ is a real and viable option in a radically secular world.

A Few Caveats

Why care about cultural apologetics? Because we love Jesus and our neighbors. This tool deserves to be pulled from the toolkit and used. Of course, as we engage in this method, we should mention a few caveats, since every tool has its positive and negative sides.

16. Taylor, *Secular Age*, 304.
17. Rodney Stark, *The Rise of Christianity: How the Obscure, Marginal Jesus Movement Became the Dominant Religious Force in the Western World in a Few Centuries* (1996; repr., San Francisco: HarperSanFrancisco, 1997), 18.

One caution in prioritizing cultural apologetics is that the *culture* part can dwarf the *apologetic* part. By so emphasizing study of the culture or the society you're called to reach, you may become underdeveloped in studying the Scriptures. You can lose sight of the reason you're engaging in the task in the first place: to foster a missionary encounter with others. And not just an encounter or dialogue but a gospel-shaped missionary moment where, yes, you find areas of common ground on which to build, but then you tackle the areas of conflict, where the gospel's offense must remain.

Another risk in prioritizing cultural apologetics is that you so focus on understanding the people you're trying to reach that you tailor the presentation of Christianity *only* to the needs and questions they already have. You try to fit Christianity into another framework of thought, showing how it answers and fulfills people's longings. As a starting point, this is fine. I've heard it said we're to listen carefully for the questions being asked in each generation and then show how the gospel answers those questions. That's good, but it doesn't go far enough. Faithfulness to the gospel means we don't merely answer the questions people in society are asking—we also raise questions people should be asking but aren't. The gospel upends all earthly and cultural scripts and frameworks, at least at some level. The gospel presses different questions. The risk with cultural apologetics could be that the cultural trends and questions drive everything and the challenge that Christianity poses to the world gets muted.

One last caveat, perhaps the most important: We mustn't be so faithless as to think the gospel needs cultural Christianity or cultural apologetics to remain the power of God unto salvation. The church before Christendom wasn't propped up by cultural Christianity, and Christians in many parts of the world today walk with God just fine with no need for cultural crutches. Yes, Christendom may be an asset to Christianity in terms of plausibility structures, making it a live wire in a sociological sense. But theologically, we must never assume cultural Christianity supplies the electricity. It's the Spirit who makes the gospel spread like wildfire, blowing when and where he pleases.

Conversion is always impossible without supernatural intervention. Cultural Christianity may be one of the tools God uses to smooth the path so some will understand the basics of biblical truth before being confronted with Christ's specific claims. But God doesn't depend on Christendom, and we shouldn't either. Whether we labor in fields where Christianity seems as far-fetched a possibility as becoming Zoroastrian, or whether we labor in areas that still bear the fragrance of commonly held Christian values, our call to evangelism and missions remains the same—even if certain methods must change based on cultural context.

No matter what approaches we suggest or methods we use, we mustn't forget that in the end, the primary reason anyone believes the implausible testimony that Jesus of Nazareth walked out of his grave isn't because of live or dead wires, traditional or cultural apologetics, or our expertise in sharing the gospel. The reason is the Spirit's awakening.

2

A Biblical Vision

CHRISTOPHER WATKIN

Christianity is our world. . . . Our whole science, everything that passes through our head, has inevitably gone through this history.

—CARL JUNG, BASEL SEMINAR, 1934[1]

In the movie *The Bourne Identity*, Jason Bourne is an amnesiac, traveling across Europe and feeling drawn to certain locations without understanding why.[2] In one scene, he visits a Paris apartment that, according to his documents, is registered in his name. Although he has no recollection of the place, he experiences brief flashbacks to when he used to live there. The apartment is familiar

1. In C. G. Jung, *Psychological Reflections. A New Anthology of His Writings, 1905–1961*, ed. Jolande Jacobi (Princeton, NJ: Princeton University Press, 1973), 341.
2. *The Bourne Identity*, directed by Doug Liman, 2002, Universal Pictures.

but also strange; it is home but also a home of which he has no memory. Eventually (and if you haven't seen the Bourne movies, this is a spoiler alert, and I advise you to skip to the next paragraph now), he learns he has been to these places as a covert operative, but his memories were erased as part of a clandestine government program designed to create highly effective, morally unencumbered assassins.

The British historian Tom Holland is—I hope he wouldn't mind me saying—no Jason Bourne. But his experience is remarkably similar. In his book *Dominion*, Holland testifies to a feeling not unlike the one that crept up on Bourne in that Paris apartment. From a boy, he was always fascinated by the cultures of ancient Greece and Rome: their heroic battles, mighty heroes, and squabbling gods. But the longer he studied classical antiquity, "the more alien I found the moral certainties of the classical world."[3] Like Bourne in his Paris apartment, Holland found himself in a Christian tradition of strange familiarity:

> For a millennium and more, the civilisation into which I had been born was Christendom. Assumptions that I had grown up with—about how a society should properly be organised, and the principles that it should uphold—were not bred of classical antiquity, still less of "human nature," but very distinctively of that civilisation's Christian past.[4]

He knew that Christianity felt familiar, though he wouldn't have called it home.

What's going on here? Many things, no doubt, but among them we find a fascinating window into the stakes of cultural apologetics in the second quarter of the twenty-first century. The Bible—which is, after all, the source of these beliefs and values Holland found so

3. Tom Holland, *Dominion: How the Christian Revolution Remade the World* (New York: Basic, 2019), 17.
4. Holland, *Dominion*, 17.

uncannily familiar—is neither utterly alien nor completely familiar in the contemporary West. To adapt C. S. Lewis's imagery from "The Weight of Glory," it's the familiar scent of a flower we have never smelled, the echo of a much-loved tune we have never heard, or well-known news from a country we have never visited.[5] In this chapter, I will explore some of the Bible's alien familiarity and suggest how biblical patterns can draw late-modern people back to the home they never realized they had left.

The Bible: Pattern of Our Culture's Experience

Here's a challenge: You have to sum up the Bible, but you only have four words to do so. What will you choose? "God loved the world"? "Jesus died for you"? These and other similar formulations contain wonderful biblical truths, but they're not quite so good at capturing the rhythm of the biblical story. At the risk of coming over as rather boring, let me suggest another four words: "creation, fall, redemption, consummation."[6] Not quite as catchy, I'll grant you, but in these four words we have, compressed like a tightly coiled spring, a whole understanding of life, the world, and humanity.

Everything the Bible addresses it sees as part of this grand story of God's creation of a good world, the fall into sin, God's heroic and ferociously patient rescue mission, and the consummation of all things in the new heaven and the new earth. Everything the Christian thinks about and feels—relationships, the natural world,

5. See C. S. Lewis, *The Weight of Glory: And Other Addresses* (1949; repr., New York: HarperOne, 2001), 31.

6. The terminology of "creation, fall, redemption" is most commonly associated with mid-twentieth century Dutch Reformed theology, though similar schemata can be traced at least as far back as Augustine. Theologian Herman Dooyeweerd describes the distinctiveness of a Christian view of the world in terms of the CFR schema in *Roots of Western Culture: Pagan, Secular and Christian Options* (Toronto: Wedge, 1979). See also Herman Bavinck, *Reformed Ethics*, vol. 1, *Created, Fallen, and Converted Humanity* (Grand Rapids: Baker, 2019). For a detailed discussion of the schema, see Thomas Boston, *Human Nature in its Fourfold State* (Edinburgh: Banner of Truth, 1964).

politics, work, hobbies, triumph, tragedy, boredom—is part of this four-stage story.

It's a subtle and sophisticated story, with deep implications for the way Christians engage in cultural apologetics today. We could no doubt go on for hundreds of pages about the implications of these four short words for Christian cultural engagement,[7] but here I want to show how they can function as a lens of cultural apologetics and as a way to invite people back to a home they haven't realized they left.

Let's begin with the first two great moments of the biblical story: creation and fall. At the risk of trying your patience, let me point out that Genesis 3 comes after Genesis 1. In other words, the creation of a good world and the spoiling of that good world aren't the same event. Things haven't always been as they are now, and our current status quo was not God's original design. As a result, Christians should have no trouble accounting for the bewildering diversity of human behavior. Human beings can behave like angels when they travel across the world to help those who are struggling for life or across the street to help someone who is struggling with their shopping. But we can also be vile to each other, really quite unspeakably vile, for no other apparent purpose than the pleasure of being vile and inflicting suffering. That's quite a spectrum of behavior!

Almost all philosophies and views of humanity outside the Bible tend to overemphasize one of these realities in a way that diminishes and betrays the other. This seesawing from one view of human nature to its opposite seems to be hardwired into Western modernity. On one side, we have the gloomy account of Thomas Hobbes (1588–1679) in *Leviathan*,[8] perhaps the founding text of modern Western political thought.[9] For Hobbes, all you need to know about human

7. See Christoher Watkin, *Biblical Critical Theory: How the Bible's Unfolding Story Makes Sense of Modern Life and Culture* (Grand Rapids: Zondervan Academic, 2022).
8. Thomas Hobbes, *Leviathan* (1651; repr., Cambridge: Cambridge University Press, 1996).
9. See Gordon Hull, *Hobbes and the Making of Modern Political Thought* (London: Continuum, 2009).

behavior is summed up in three traits: We fear each other, compete with each other, and want glory and recognition for ourselves, usually at the expense of others.[10] Every act of seeming altruism is a ruse to bolster our own reputation.

On the other end of the spectrum, we have Jean-Jacques Rousseau (1712–78), an equally pivotal figure in the development of modern thought. For the Rousseau of the *Discourse on Inequality*, human beings have only two fundamental characteristics: a desire to preserve their own life and natural sentiment of pity that causes them to sympathize with the suffering of others.[11] But modern society with its inequalities, hectic rhythms, and ethos of competition bludgeons this pity out of us, replacing it with a rather Hobbesian desire to be seen as better than other people.

These fundamental dispositions, or variants of them, play themselves out in modern political and social life. Are people essentially scheming brutes who need to be kept in check by the strong hand of authority? Or are they bruised flowers that need nurturing so they can express their true selves? In one important sense, our politics can be understood in terms of radically different answers to the question of human nature.

So where does cultural apologetics come in? I suspect most people, if you asked them, wouldn't be quite as radical as either Rousseau or Hobbes. We have a gut instinct that people can be extraordinarily benevolent and kind for reasons that can't always be traced back to self-promotion or personal gain. And we have a sense that the capacity for human evil and self-destruction is almost unlimited and that there are no depths to which we will not sink if given half a chance. The problem is that, unless there is a distinction between the origin of good and the origin of evil, it is extraordinarily hard to account for the vast range encompassed by those two views

10. Hobbes, *Leviathan*, 88.
11. Jean-Jacques Rousseau, *The Discourses and Other Early Political Writings*, ed. Victor Gourevitch (Cambridge: Cambridge University Press, 1997) 152, 218.

of human nature. We can feel it as a gut instinct, and we can show examples of both sorts of behavior, but when it comes to explaining and justifying our feelings about its great diversity, we find it hard indeed. That is why our theories tend to gravitate to one of the two extremes, even if lived experience holds both together.

So when Christians explain the biblical pattern of creation and fall to a secular and skeptical late modernity, we're not entering enemy territory. We're inviting wanderers back home to a view of the world that can make sense of both the best and the worst of humanity. In short, the Bible makes sense of us. It makes better sense of us than we can make of ourselves.

This is the great and endlessly rich argument of Augustine's *City of God*, still the single most important book of cultural apologetics outside the Bible.[12] Augustine holds up the sort of mirror to late Roman culture that you find in professional makeup salons, flooding the subject's face with a penetrating light that shows every tiny imperfection, bump, and crevice. He shows how Rome can't quite make sense of itself and that, if it cares to look, the biblical story of creation, fall, redemption, and consummation accounts for the oddness and tensions Rome tries to brush under the carpet.

One major lesson cultural apologists can learn from *The City of God*—a lesson that is simple to express but takes a lifetime to explore—is that the Bible itself is the apologetic. It's the shape of the biblical story, expressed most simply and sparsely in the four moments of creation, fall, redemption, and consummation, and also a rich, multilayered, and exceedingly complex story as we delve into its details. It's the story of reality, the story of the universe in which we actually happen to live, that does the apologetic heavy lifting.

We don't need a command of the latest sociological theories to be good cultural apologists. We don't need complex philosophical concepts (and I write as a philosopher!) to be incisive, relevant,

12. Augustine, *The City of God*, trans. R. W. Dyson (Cambridge: Cambridge University Press, 1998).

thought-provoking, and tantalizing cultural apologists. These things can sometimes help, of course, and they certainly have their place in the ecosystem of cultural apologetics. But that ecosystem is—or at least should be—fundamentally and ultimately Bible-shaped and Bible-rhythmed. Christian cultural apologetics is biblical apologetics.

The Gospel: Subversive Fulfillment of Our Culture's Desire

Let's now turn from the overall pattern of the biblical story line and consider one passage in some detail. In 1 Corinthians 1, Paul rolls up his sleeves and gets down and dirty in the business of cultural apologetics. In four paradigm-defining verses (vv. 22–25), he gives a thoroughly biblical blueprint for the cultural apologist.

In verse 22, Paul identifies some of the deep longings and values of the two major cultures of his first-century world: "Jews demand signs and Greeks seek wisdom." It becomes clear later in the passage that the Jews want a demonstration of divine power. At this point, a short-circuited cultural apologetics would jump immediately to saying something like, "So come and find the power and the wisdom you are looking for in Christ: He is the all-powerful one, the all-wise one; find all your desires satisfied in him." But not Paul. He claims in verse 23 to be offering the precise opposite of what the Jews and Greeks are looking for: "But we preach Christ crucified, a stumbling block to Jews and folly to Gentiles." You may be looking for power, dear Jews, but I come only with the weakness of a man gasping for breath in shame, dying a death reserved for the worst sort of criminal. And you say you want wisdom, you Greeks, but I'm afraid I come to you with a message of foolishness: Here you'll find no august, toga-clad orator crafting fine sentences, but a man stripped naked on the cross, hardly able to speak at all. You who want strength, come and find weakness. You who desire wisdom, come and find foolishness. The word of the cross thwarts, confounds, and subverts the cherished values of cultures.

But Paul hasn't finished: "But to those whom God has called, both Jews and Greeks, Christ the power of God and the wisdom of God. For the foolishness of God is wiser than human wisdom, and the weakness of God is stronger than human strength" (vv. 24–25 NIV). What? Hasn't Paul just made painfully, provocatively clear that the word of the cross is weak and foolish? How can the cross be God's power and God's wisdom? How can it be wiser than human wisdom and stronger than human strength, all the while remaining weak in the eyes of the Jews and foolish in the eyes of the Greeks? This is the brilliance of the cross: It most certainly fulfills the desires and values of the cultures of the ancient Near East but only on the condition that it also, and at the same time, confounds and subverts them.

Let's put these two together. It's as if Paul is saying to the Jews and the Greeks: There is a power to be found and a wisdom to seek, but you are looking for them in all the wrong places. As one of our own poets has said, we have run, we have crawled, we have scaled these city walls, but we still haven't found what we're looking for. You Jews, you Greeks, are you truly serious about searching for wisdom, about seeking power? Are you so serious that you could swallow your pride and contemplate looking for them in the place you think you would be least likely to find them? I know it sounds odd, perverse even, but here is God's promise to you: If you are willing to let go of your narrow and culturally specific preconception of what wisdom must surely look like, of what form power must surely take, if you leave those preconceptions at the foot of the cross and receive the weak power and foolish wisdom of God, then you'll find power and wisdom—the richness, depth, and intensity of which you cannot even currently imagine—because you'll know the One who isn't merely wise but is wisdom (Prov. 8; Col. 2:3) and the One who not only is powerful but from whom all power derives and to whom it answers (1 Chron. 29:11–12; Col. 1:16–17).

Taking Paul's masterful presentation of the cross as our pattern, what lessons can we draw for cultural apologetics today? I can think of three.

First, both the Christians who have nothing but scorn and condemnation for late-modern culture and also the Christians who want nothing more than to get alongside the culture and show how the gospel is relevant to it are onto something. But they only have part of the story and, for that reason, distort the whole story. The word of the cross confronts our culture's great values of freedom and equality, just as it confronted the Greek value of wisdom and the Jewish value of power. But it also radically fulfills those values, breaking them down and rebuilding them in the process, setting their castles in the air on the firm foundation of God's character.[13]

Second, cultural apologetics is cruciform. Paul doesn't feel the need to stray into the niceties of first-century philosophy before unloading both barrels of his cultural apologetic salvo. We know from elsewhere in his writing that he was no stranger to Greek poets and ideas (e.g., Acts 17:28; 1 Cor. 15:33; Titus 1:12). But in this passage, he elaborates a profound and incisive posture of cultural critique by pressing into the cross, not by hiding it away in a closet for fear of what people might think. I concluded the previous section with the affirmation that Christian cultural apologetics is biblical apologetics. The message resounding in 1 Corinthians 1 is that Christian cultural apologetics is cruciform apologetics; we learn how to engage

13. The term *subversive fulfillment* is theological in origin, appearing in the work of Dutch missiologist Hendrik Kraemer (1888–1965), "Continuity or Discontinuity," in *The Authority of Faith: International Missionary Council Meeting at Tambaram, Madras*, ed. G. Paton (Oxford: Oxford University Press, 1939), 5. See also Daniel Strange, "For Their Rock Is Not as Our Rock: The Gospel as the 'Subversive Fulfillment' of the Religious Other," *Journal of the Evangelical Theological Society* 56, no. 2 (2013): 391–92. On Strange's development of subversive fulfillment, see also chap. 5 of this book.

with, subvert, and fulfill the ambient cultural values of our age not by sidestepping the cross but by diving into the depths of its wisdom and power, and coming up with their treasure. The heart of cultural apologetics is the heart of the gospel.

Third and finally, the cultural apologist can take from 1 Corinthians 1 a humble confidence in the power and plans of God. The chapter is remarkably well-written and well-constructed, with its repeated motifs and rhythms, its crescendos and unexpected turns. But Paul doesn't put his confidence in his mastery of Greek and his command of the ideas he is conjuring with, though these are evident for all to see. The baseline of hope that thumps and hums throughout this passage doesn't beat out the rhythm of clever human arguments. In fact, we'd be hard pressed to find any passage in the Bible that is more ruthlessly and relentlessly critical of such arguments than this one.

Yet Paul is hopeful. He is hopeful because "it pleased God through the folly of what we preach to save those who believe" (v. 21), and he is hopeful because Christ crucified is "to those who are called, both Jews and Greeks, Christ the power of God and the wisdom of God" (v. 24). As we labor in the field of cultural apologetics, Paul reminds us that this ministry is no different from any other in that it relies utterly, desperately, on the grace and power of God. But my goodness: what grace, and what power!

The End of All Our Exploring

Both the creation-fall-redemption-consummation pattern of the biblical story line and Paul's approach to cultural apologetics in 1 Corinthians 1 remind today's budding cultural apologists that they are neither calling people to something utterly foreign to their experience, nor calling them to find the fulfillment of their deepest values and longings in the way they understand that fulfillment today. Like the unbidden flashbacks that haunt Jason Bourne as he scours the world searching for who he really is, like the nagging sense in Tom Holland's mind, insisting that the world in which he belongs is Bible-shaped, cultural apologists are an insistent whisperer. In our late-modern culture, we hold out a Bible and speak softly to all who will listen, "You belong here, though not in the way you think." We don't call late moderns to stop asking the big questions or to settle into a state of being comfortably numb. We call them to the quest beautifully captured towards the end of T. S. Eliot's *Little Gidding*, where we read that, at the end of all our exploration, we return to where we started and yet know the place for the first time.[14] To know the place, yes, but also to know the One who made the place; to know power but also to know the One in whom all power rests; to know wisdom but also to know the One who is wisdom.

Often, cultural apologists call people to a reality that is odder, more challenging, and more enchanting than the alternatives. Odder because, as G. K. Chesterton captures so well in *Orthodoxy*, all the bulges and ungainly lumps of Christianity are there for a reason, because they make it fit with a reality that is itself far from smooth and transparent. Take one of them away, and the edifice begins to totter:

> Christianity was like a huge and ragged and romantic rock, which, though it sways on its pedestal at a touch, yet, because its exaggerated excrescences exactly balance each other, is enthroned there for a thousand years. In a Gothic cathedral the columns were all different, but they were all necessary. Every support seemed an accidental and fantastic support; every buttress was a flying buttress. So in Christendom apparent accidents are balanced.[15]

The Bible fits the human condition like a glove. But gloves aren't perfectly symmetrical; none of the fingers is quite the same size,

14. T. S. Eliot, *Four Quartets* (New York: Harcourt Brace, 1943), 39.
15. G. K. Chesterton, *Orthodoxy* (New York: Allen Lane, 1909), 180.

and the thumb seems to be off doing its own thing on the side. All the irregularity and lopsidedness of a glove is no mere indulgence or obtuse flight of fancy. Every kink, every strange angle, every ungainly protuberance is there for a reason, and they are all there for the same reason: to fit the human hand.

To weary and heavy-burdened late moderns, as well as ambitious and motivated late moderns, depressed and struggling late moderns, and just plain old average late moderns, the cultural apologist's message is consistent: Go on, try the Bible on for size. You may well find, perhaps to your surprise, that it fits like a glove.

3

A Framework for Retrieval

JOSHUA D. CHATRAW

Non-Christians are "not abstractions; they're either Greek non-Christians, or Jewish non-Christians, or Buddhist non-Christians or something. And so apologetics is automatically contextualization."

Timothy Keller made this comment to me several years ago as we talked apologetics in his New York City office.[1] Another way to put what Tim was getting at that day is to say apologetics shouldn't be conceived as a purely theoretical discipline, detached from the specificities of different sociohistorical settings. Understanding context—which includes cultural narratives, institutions, and artifacts as well as the way these realities shape people's values, aspirations, patterns of life, and plausibility structures[2]—is vital for effective and faithful apologetics.

1. This conversation took place on December 11, 2017.
2. "Plausibility structures" is a concept that relates to how we are inclined to believe something based on the people we are surrounded by and the cultural situation we find ourselves in. See Peter L. Berger, *The Sacred Canopy: Elements of a Sociological Theory of Religion* (1967; repr., New York: Anchor, 1990), 45.

Since I've made this opening point, it would be understandable for a reader to assume I would gladly affirm the label "cultural apologetics." But for the sake of transparency, I need to make what might amount to a surprising confession: I have some concerns.

First, adding the adjective "cultural" to "apologetics" could wrongly suggest it is possible to do apologetics from a location outside of culture to a generic other. In contrast to a theoretical and acultural view of the discipline, apologetics is practiced not in the abstract but in the particular. We're always speaking to specific persons with their own culturally embedded stories. Hence, all apologetics is cultural apologetics because all persuasion occurs within a specific culture, addressing a culture's specific challenges.[3] Even at basic levels of communication and plausibility structures, the languages and "rationalities" at work in debate are themselves tied to particular contexts.[4]

The question isn't if someone is doing "cultural apologetics" but how aware apologists are of their own cultural assumptions as well as the assumptions of the context in which their appeals are being heard. The question isn't if people are wrapped up in the rationalities of their historical context or narratives of a culture but how well apologists are studying their context to leverage its opportunities for persuasion and to respond to its unique challenges.

The practical risk of using this label is that it forms two tribes: "apologists" versus "cultural apologists." This divide could encourage "cultural apologists" (to their detriment) to sidestep historical, scientific, and precise arguments. And the label "cultural apologetics" could leave "apologists" wrongly imagining they are doing *noncultural*

3. Joshua D. Chatraw and Mark D. Allen, *The Augustine Way: Retrieving a Vision for the Church's Apologetic Witness* (Grand Rapids: Baker Academic, 2023), 35–69.

4. By "rationalities" I am not denying basic universal logic. Instead, I am referring to the larger rival conceptions of rationality that undergird the acceptance or denial of various theories in different disciplines or in different cultures. For more on this, see Alister MacIntyre, *Whose Justice? Which Rationality?* (Notre Dame, IN: University of Notre Dame Press, 1988); Alister McGrath, *The Territories of Human Reason: Science and Theology in the Age of Multiple Rationalities* (Oxford: Oxford University Press, 2019).

apologetics—providing universal proofs for the truth of Christianity that can simply be plugged and played in any context because their persuasive power is immune from the changing winds of culture.[5] However, because culture shapes how people reason and what they find true, good, and beautiful, those in ministry who have only been trained in "apologetics" without learning how to integrate cultural analysis into their approach can often be frustrated by the gap between the approach they were taught and the actual tools needed to understand and persuade in their ministry contexts.

At this point, it would be fair to wonder what I am doing writing a chapter in a book with the subtitle *An Introduction to Cultural Apologetics*! The short answer is that I still agree with the comment Keller made years ago: "Apologetics is automatically contextualization." I support the overall approach Collin Hansen describes in the introduction to this book with his emphasis on cultural assumptions, narrative, historical analysis, and an account of humans as worshipers—while remaining concerned that the label *cultural apologetics* could raise new problems.

My second worry with the label *cultural apologetics* is that the terminology has only recently begun to gain traction and only within certain evangelical circles. Thus, its usage runs the risk of sounding as if those who adopt this approach are doing something new.[6] To this perception, this chapter serves as a response. For while the label is relatively new, the ideas animating this book's chapters are far from a flash in the pan. Rather, they find precedent in significant apologists within the Christian tradition. In support of this claim, this chapter will sample contributions by three influential apologists.

5. That the contributors to this volume use various types of arguments for Christianity in their different works, including those sometimes labeled as *classical* and *evidential* arguments, as Keller did himself, further calls into question any neat distinction between "apologetics" and "cultural apologetics."
6. For an example of this kind of claim by a prominent apologist, see William Lane Craig, *Reasonable Faith: Christian Truth and Apologetics*, 3rd ed. (Wheaton: Crossway, 2008), 65.

Augustine: Paragon of Early Apologists to the Pagans

Stephen Presley documents how the early church developed for apologetic purposes "the full set of rhetorical devices" they inherited from their cultural setting.[7] Responding to challenges of their particular context, early apologists "defended the uniqueness of Christianity, argued that Christian doctrine and morality were more intellectually satisfying than the alternatives, appealed to the antiquity of Christianity, and showed how Christianity served the public good."[8] Presley describes how early apologists used a strategy of both/and: "assimilating"/"conquering." Surveying works by apologists such as Justin Martyr, Origen, and Aristides, Presley illustrates how these authors used their cultures' rhetorical tools and forms of argumentation while simultaneously critiquing their competitors' views to argue for Christianity's truth and goodness.[9]

Similarly, John Cavadini notes the dynamic and contextual nature of the early Christian apologies in contrast to the tendency of later theologians to interpret these apologies anachronistically by way of their own systematic theologies:

> In such a context [i.e., of the early church], it is probably better to talk about strategies of persuasion, of the use of shared rhetorical convention and philosophical wisdom, to help leverage and secure Christian commitment, rather than to think in terms of the contrast between "natural" and "revealed" theology that has more of a place in later systematic or scholastic theology. . . . It may be that our readiness to use such categories as "natural knowledge of God" anachronistically has blinded us to the genius of these

7. Stephen O. Presley, *Cultural Sanctification: Engaging the World Like the Early Church* (Grand Rapids: Eerdmans, 2024), 85.
8. Presley, *Cultural Sanctification*, 85.
9. Presley, *Cultural Sanctification*, 91.

> ancient strategies of persuasion and clarification, and kept us from learning as much as we can from them.[10]

Asking which of the modern categories (e.g., presuppositional, evidential, cultural) the early apologists fit within is like asking what the early church thought about a liberal democracy. Attempting to answer such questions framed in anachronistic categories keeps us from a deeper understanding as well as a faithful retrieval of their work.

Of all the early apologists, Augustine serves as a paragon for our purposes, in part because, as Gerard O'Daly shows, many of his arguments were retrieved from his predecessors' writings and then creatively contextualized for a different situation.[11] "The post-Constantinian Christianization of the Roman empire," O'Daly argues, "had altered the context of apologetic. Rome had a new public religion, and the question of its efficacy in protecting Rome called for new arguments. Yet many elements of earlier apologetic could be, and were, exploited by Augustine."[12] Augustine was conscious of the universal longings and fears of the human heart. However, he also understood how cultivating desires and doubts hinges on historical factors. For example, the immediate occasion for *The City of God* was the sack of Rome and the pastoral and apologetic concerns this event triggered. With Rome in rubble, it was not just the future of the empire that was in question. Because many Christians had put their hope for the kingdom of God *by way* of the Roman Empire, the sack called into question the church's legitimacy and future. In the days following Rome's fall, pagan traditionalists escaped to Augustine's

10. John C. Cavadini, *Visioning Augustine: Challenges in Contemporary Theology* (Oxford: Wiley-Blackwell, 2019), 241.
11. The rest of this section is a highly compressed summary of some of the themes explored in Chatraw and Allen, *The Augustine Way*.
12. Gerard O'Daly, *Augustine's City of God: A Reader's Guide* (New York: Oxford University Press, 1999), 39. Later, O'Daly adds, "Thus, while Augustine undoubtedly borrows themes and arguments from the earlier apologists and related literature, no one of his precursors has either a dominant or a profound influence on his apologetic concerns and strategies" (52).

North Africa and blamed Christians for the empire's decline. These attacks by strident pagans added to the anxiety many Christians felt during this time of tectonic shifts and an uncertain future.[13]

With these particular concerns in view, Augustine wrote his apologetic magnum opus with three groups in mind: pagan critics, former confessing Christians, and Christians who had begun to waver under the "weight of the Roman religious and political tradition which represented Christianity as a betrayal of all that had made Rome great and, most especially, as a betrayal of its gods."[14] Augustine's response engaged history, challenged the assumptions of their particular social location, and offered a theologically nuanced way to live within the emerging situation.

His meta-approach in *The City of God* was to out-narrate the voices who accused Christianity of being harmful to the welfare of the empire and her citizens. In the first ten books, Augustine offered an immanent critique against his rivals, using the pagans' own authorities—narrating a deflationary account of their history. In the second half (books 11–22), Augustine invited readers to try on the biblical story, arguing along the way that Christianity makes sense of history, the human experience, and the material world.

Augustine's biblical vision equipped him with the resources to critique Roman society's social underpinnings. Without completely denying the relative value of earthly goods, his biblical eschatology furnished Augustine with a vantage point that transcended and critiqued the myths and ultimate aims of the Roman Empire. But as recent scholars have noted, his cultural critique did not simply deconstruct. Augustine cut in order to heal.[15]

---

13. For more on Augustine's context, see Peter Brown, *Augustine of Hippo: A Biography* (Berkley: University of California Press, 2000), 441–73.
14. Babcock, introduction to *The Works of Saint Augustine*, vol. I/6, *The City of God* (1–10), ed. Boniface Ramsey, trans. William Babcock (Hyde Park, NY: New City, 2012), xiv.
15. See, e.g., Paul R. Kolbet, *Augustine and the Cure of Souls: Revising a Classical Ideal* (Notre Dame, IN: University of Notre Dame Press, 2009); Curtis Chang, *Engaging Unbelief: A Captivating Strategy from Augustine and Aquinas* (Downers Grove, IL: InterVarsity, 2000).

Augustine converted pagan and Roman aspirations—represented by such words as *peace*, *happiness*, and *justice*—to show how they are understood and fulfilled within the Christian narrative. For instance, rather than suggesting his opponents should stop seeking "happiness," Augustine provoked them to reconsider how happiness should be pursued and where it is ultimately found. The "innate goods" common in this life are temporal and our experience of them burdened by the knowledge of their eventual loss: "The life, therefore, which is weighed down by the burden of such great and severe evils, or is subject to the chance that such great and severe evils might afflict it, should by no means be called happy."[16] Hence, Augustine challenged his readers to consider the possibility of another kind of happiness:

> If anyone uses this life in such a way that he directs it to that other life as the end which he loves with ardent intensity and for which he hopes with unwavering faithfulness, it is not absurd to call him happy even now, although happy in hope rather than in this reality. Without that hope, in fact, this reality is only a false happiness and a great misery. For it does not make use of the true goods of the soul, because no wisdom is true wisdom if it does not direct its intention—in everything that it discerns with prudence, bears with fortitude, constrains with temperance, and distributes with justice—to the end where God will be all in all in assured eternity and perfect peace.[17]

His interaction with the concept of happiness is an example of an important feature of Augustine's persuasive strategy. He entered the dominant cultural narratives of his day to offer a severe diagnosis. But then, as a good doctor, he offered the medicine of Jesus Christ and reassured his patients that if the gospel is humbly received, their personal stories would be redeemed and their desires healed.

16. Augustine, *The City of God*, 19.4.
17. Augustine, *The City of God*, 19.20.

Blaise Pascal: Apologist to an Emerging Dechristianized World

In a commentary on Blaise Pascal's *Pensées*, Peter Kreeft writes, "Most Christian apologetics today is still written from a medieval mind-set in one sense: as if we still lived in a Christian culture, a Christian civilization, a society that reinforced the Gospel. No. The honeymoon is over. The Middle Ages are over." Kreeft makes this point about the present in support of his argument for Pascal's uniqueness and relevance for today: "[Pascal] is the first to realize the new dechristianized, desacramentalized world and to address it."[18]

Pascal's apologetic was designed to respond to at least two intellectual streams within early-modern France. The first current was led by the influential essayist Michel de Montaigne, who died thirty years before Pascal's birth. In response to the religious wars that ravaged Europe, Montaigne diagnosed the root cause to be strong conviction and certainty; he saw both as fueling violence and undermining the simple joys of life. For Montaigne, the attempt to ascertain sacred truth was a fool's errand. Viewing religious truth as a byproduct of geography and history, Montaigne was skeptical that it could be deciphered by mere humans. Thus, he reasoned, it is better to not get carried away by religious passion and to instead live lightly, enjoying the simple pleasures. While formally remaining Catholic, Montaigne imbibed a type of skepticism that gave up on the possibility of rationally supporting answers to life's big questions. Rather than passionately pursuing transcendent answers, he thought, one should pursue "immanent contentment."[19]

The second Frenchman, a contemporary of Pascal, is the father of modern philosophy himself, René Descartes. Descartes was appalled

18. Peter Kreeft, *Christianity for Modern Pagans: Pascal's Pensées* (San Francisco: Ignatius, 1993), 12–13. See also Blaise Pascal, *Pensées*, trans. A. J. Krailsheimer (New York: Penguin, 1995).
19. Benjamin Storey and Jenna Silber Storey, *Why We Are Restless: On the Modern Quest for Contentment* (Princeton, NJ: Princeton University Press, 2021), 33.

by Montaignian skepticism. In response to the emerging insecurity about past certainties, Descartes developed an innovative approach to achieve certitude. His strategy was to sequester himself to only his thoughts and methodologically doubt everything. The only thing he couldn't doubt, he reasoned, was that he was thinking. From here, he assembled an argument that in his mind led to proof that God existed. This Cartesian inward turn, an attempt to isolate oneself from contingencies and to prove truth autonomously, contributed to a modern way of thinking that emphasized reason as the final and ultimate authority, while minimizing truth rooted in tradition or revelation.

Both Montaigne's and Descartes's ideas were absorbed into the air that many of Pascal's contemporaries breathed. This cultural atmosphere, which Kreeft alludes to as "dechristianized" and "desacramentalized," demanded an apologetic approach sensitive to these changing conditions.

For Pascal, the logic of the heart—which included truth, beauty, and goodness—is ingrained in each human. This logic includes instinctive first principles, which cannot be proven in the way one proves a math problem. Instead, they are realities we assume and are meant to reason from—space, time, and motion as well as faith, hope, and love. While Pascal gave reasons for faith, he also maintained that the logic of the heart goes beyond the reductionistic epistemology spurred on by Descartes. So rather than attempting to strip the mind of everything that was not certain and arguing by way of methodological doubt to "prove" God's existence, Pascal's apologetic was framed by a more capacious account of rationality. Moreover, because he observed that his contemporaries mocked and hated religion, to "cure" them he advocated for an approach that first argues Christianity should be respected, especially due to its explanatory power concerning human nature.[20] Second, he moved to

20. Pascal, *Pensées*, 4. Like Augustine, Pascal uses medicinal language, and his approach also can appropriately be described as therapeutic. For connections between Pascal and Augustine, see James R. Peters, *The Logic of the Heart: Augustine, Pascal, and the*

convince others they should want Christianity to be true: "Make it attractive, make good men wish it were true." Finally, the case should be made that Christianity is indeed true.[21]

Pascal believed Montaigne was dreadfully wrong about human nature—we're both great and wretched. Humans will remain restless if we fight against our instincts to rise above a trivial life. Pascal argued that by settling for skepticism and attempting to convince ourselves that the fleeting happiness found in this world's pleasures is enough, Montaigne's posture would blind humans from reality and leave them in despair. Montaigne's way of life would only, in the end, make us more miserable. Benjamin and Jenna Storey sum up Pascal's point: "Our consciousness of our mortality and our awareness of our own ignorance makes us unhappy; we cannot learn to die, or rest our well-made heads on the pillow of ignorance, as Montaigne hopes. No psychic equilibrium is possible for a being whose desires so radically outstrip his possibilities. Misery follows ineluctably from an honest estimate of the gap between what we want and what we are."[22]

Pascal believed that those who followed Montaigne's approach were formed to find Christianity hard to believe. Within this context, Pascal famously proposed his "Wager." His goal was to wake people up from the stupor brought by diversions. Having sneered at any chance to find confidence in sacred truths, they had diverted their attention to worldly pleasures. *After all*, we can imagine them thinking, *since we can't really know, why not just avoid betting and tend to our gardens and playfully enjoy life as it comes.* In essence Pascal responds, "But isn't that still a bet? And consider what one gains by betting on God versus what one stands to lose if one bets on worldly pleasures and God turns out to exist!" This wasn't meant to be a universal argument that *proves* God's existence. Instead, it was an

Rationality of Faith (Grand Rapids: Baker Academic, 2009). In one sense, Pascal was retrieving Augustine for his own time and place.

21. Pascal, *Pensées*, 4 (§ 12).

22. Storey and Storey, *Why We Are Restless*, 65–66.

argument meant to persuade sinners, caught in their own pride and worldly diversions, to reconsider their life as well as the wisest way to wager on the question of God.[23]

For the person awakened to the danger of a wagering on a life of "immanent contentment" but still frozen in unbelief, Pascal famously advises, "You want to be cured of unbelief and you ask for the remedy: learn from those who were once bound like you and who now wager all they have. These are people who know the road you wish to follow, who have been cured of the affliction of which you wish to be cured: follow the way by which they began. They behaved as if they did believe, taking holy water, having masses said, and so on."[24] Pascal, aware that a person's pattern of life affects what one finds plausible to believe, incorporates this existential challenge into his apologetic.[25]

C. S. Lewis: Weaver of Apologetic Spells to the Disenchanted

European apologetics in the twentieth century was characterized by "a less structured and more fluid approach" when compared to American apologetics of the same period.[26] This is likely due in part to the lack of formal (and tribal) methodological debates and the diverse backgrounds of Europe's leading apologists. The most influential of these apologists was the literary scholar C. S. Lewis. Like our previous two apologists surveyed in this chapter, C. S. Lewis is a familiar figure whose apologetic approach is difficult to classify.

23. For more on Pascal's Wager, see Graeme Hunter, *Pascal the Philosopher: An Introduction* (Toronto: University of Toronto Press, 2013), 92–148.
24. Pascal, *Pensées*, 125.
25. For a contemporary application of Pascal's approach, see Joshua D. Chatraw and Jack Carson, *Surprised by Doubt: How Disillusionment Can Invite Us to a Deeper Faith* (Grand Rapids: Brazos, 2023), 125–62.
26. Benjamin K. Forrest, Joshua D. Chatraw, and Alister E. McGrath, *The History of Apologetics: A Biographical and Methodological Introduction* (Grand Rapids: Zondervan Academic, 2019), 539.

Alister McGrath rightly emphasizes that those "who assign [Lewis] to some predetermined 'school' of thought end up distorting his approach, which resists the conveniences of categorization."[27]

Lewis was acutely aware of the cultural assumptions that needed to be challenged in his twentieth-century intellectual milieu, specifically reductive materialism, which he had himself once embraced as a rationalistic atheist, as well as a "chronology snobbery," which looked down upon ancient ways of thinking. He saw his society as needing to be awakened "from the evil enchantment of worldliness which has been laid upon us for nearly a hundred years." His apologetic response was to try "to weave a spell" to break this enchantment.[28] For our purposes, two characteristics of his approach stand out.

First, Lewis stressed the importance of what today is often referred to as contextualization. For example, he underscored the apologist's role as presenting "that which is timeless in the particular language of our own day." We do this, he explained, by learning "the language of our audience" and then translating concepts and ideas in culturally relatable and illuminating ways.[29] Lewis modeled the work of theological translation for the everyday person in his most influential apologetic work, *Mere Christianity*, which was originally a series of radio addresses for BBC during World War II. The various genres he used as an apologist, designed to speak to different people in different ways, are examples of Lewis recontextualizing similar ideas for diverse audiences. While Lewis routinely sought to undermine logical positivism and reenchant the disenchanted, he did this by way of a remarkable diversity of genres: fictional demonic letters (*Screwtape Letters*), oral lectures (which became *The Abolition of Man*), direct apologetic discourse (*Miracles*), children's literature (The Chronicles of Narnia), a fictional supposal of the afterlife (*The*

27. McGrath, "C. S. Lewis: Imaginative Apologetics of a Reluctant Convert," in Forrest, Chatraw, and McGrath, *History of Apologetics*, 616.
28. C. S. Lewis, *The Weight of Glory* (1949; repr., San Francisco: HarperOne, 2001), 31.
29. C. S. Lewis, "Christian Apologetics," in *God in the Dock* (Grand Rapids: Eerdmans, 1970), 96.

Great Divorce), and science fiction (The Space Trilogy). While his apologetic corpus displays keen sensitivity to the needs of different audiences, his individual works are regularly marked by an attempt to "subvert some established truths of the day and expose them as shadows and illusions," while providing an alternative vision of reality.[30]

Second, Austin Farrer (1904–68), a contemporary of Lewis's at Oxford, once explained Lewis's genius in this way: He leads us to believe we're "listening to an argument," but in actuality "we are presented with a vision, and it is the vision that carries conviction."[31] This isn't to say Lewis avoided direct arguments, which are obviously evident in such works as *Mere Christianity* and *Miracles*. Yet rather than attempting to "prove" Christianity, Lewis supported its rationality through the vision he cast. Even his narrower lines of persuasion—for example, his argument from desire—serve as threads in a larger tapestry: "If I find in myself a desire which no experience in this world can satisfy, the most probable explanation is that I was made for another world."[32] For every common human desire (hunger and thirst, for instance), something in this world fulfills this desire (food and drink). The best explanation for the common human desire for something that transcends this world is that we were made for another world. Lewis understood this desire, which outstrips anything our common experience in this world offers, not as a proof but as one clue that, when put alongside other clues, makes God's existence the best explanation.

In his fictional stories, Lewis welcomed his audiences to imaginatively "try on" Christianity. Through carefully selected images and metaphors designed to register with his audiences, he challenged the culturally assumed, one-dimensional visions of the world and invited his readers to look again through Christian lenses. Taken as a whole,

30. McGrath, "C. S. Lewis," 611.
31. Austin Farrer, "The Christian Apologist," in *Light on C. S. Lewis*, ed. Jocelyn Gibb (London: Bles, 1965), 37.
32. C. S. Lewis, *Mere Christianity* (1952; repr. New York: HarperCollins, 2001), 136–37.

his apologetic power rested in his use of reason, imagery, and narrative to cast Christianity as a way of seeing that makes best sense of the world. As Lewis famously wrote, "I believe in Christianity as I believe that the sun has risen, not only because I see it but because by it, I see everything else."[33]

The More Important Question

I noted at the beginning of this chapter that in my view, *cultural apologetics* as a term has some problems. Nevertheless, more important than the question of *what* nomenclature is best is the perennial question of *how* we will serve as apologetic witnesses.

The animating ideas of this book—its emphasis on contextualization, narrative, historical contingencies, and an account of humans as desiring beings—aren't novel. Absent space constraints, this chapter could have included more historical examples. Earlier I noted how Augustine retrieved from early apologists, which include a host of figures we could have explored further. Thomas Aquinas, the later Augustinian, with his appropriation of Aristotle within a context in which the ancient philosopher had reemerged as influential, would have added another layer of historical insight (and complexity!) to this discussion. With certain parallels to Pascal, Johann Georg Hamann's response to the German Enlightenment and his friend Immanuel Kant would have taken us down a historical path less trodden but no less relevant to the chapter's thesis. British author G. K. Chesterton—who greatly influenced Lewis's approach—would have been another figure worthy of our attention. And undoubtedly, if Tim Keller was still with us, he would tell me I should add Herman Bavinck, the theologian of the late nineteenth and early twentieth centuries who was committed to engaging the modern world within an orthodox theology and was significant in Keller's later thinking.

33. Lewis, *Weight of Glory*, 140.

Yet even within the space limits of this chapter, it is evident by surveying three prominent apologists within the history of the discipline that what this volume has labeled *cultural apologetics* should be seen as an apologetic retrieval rather than a novel invention. As eager inheritors of the wisdom found within the Christian apologetic tradition, we aim to faithfully preserve the one true faith once for all received (Jude 3) and to carefully discern how best to give a reason for the hope that is within us (1 Pet. 3:15). No matter what one decides to call it in the end, this apologetic retrieval with its historically and culturally attentive vision is vital for the renewal of the discipline.

PART 2

How Is Cultural Apologetics Done?

4

The Posture

Neither Accommodating nor Condemning

ALAN NOBLE

One of the most difficult challenges of cultural apologetics is having good posture. It's easy to be stiff-necked or a slouch. But to have a relaxed, confident, straight posture while engaging a hostile world is difficult. I once wrote an article for *The Atlantic* on the importance of Christian colleges having the political liberty to set community standards for housing and lifestyles.[1] I knew when writing this piece that if I spoke boldly, I'd be attacked online as a bigot. And I knew that if I hedged my language, I'd be denying my faith and making a poor argument. To write the article well, I had to boldly make my case while skillfully using rhetoric to invite my

1. Alan Noble, "How Conservative Christian Colleges Can Keep Their Faith: Empathize with LGBT Students," *The Atlantic*, August 17, 2016, https://www.theatlantic.com/politics/archive/2016/08/christian-colleges-lgbt/495815/.

reader to consider my perspective, knowing many would still think I was a bigot. And they did.

As we advance in an increasingly polarized age where Christian beliefs are considered not only wrong but even violent and oppressive, Christians will naturally feel pulled in one of two directions. On the one hand, they will feel pulled to slouch, to accommodate the culture, to shield non-Christians from less socially acceptable biblical teachings. On the other hand, they will feel pulled to be stiff-necked, to aggressively defend biblical teachings by condemning cultural idols and the people who worship them. Both postures are fundamentally defensive, positions of insecurity and doubt about God's sovereignty to save people in a wicked and fallen world.

I would go so far as to describe these as postures of nihilism: hopelessness that people can be persuaded by the truth. Instead, they assume we must either trick people into God's kingdom or condemn them as trapped outside that kingdom. A righteous posture of cultural apologetics has full faith in God's sovereignty, in his ability to save people through the truth. And it involves willingness to enter a cultural context to comprehend the idols of a particular people, to expose them as mute, deaf, and dumb.

The Pull of Accommodation

For many evangelicals, the greater temptation is accommodation to the culture. In cultural apologetics, we enter a cultural context, identify an idolatrous narrative as false, and reveal how that idol is an empty promise. Then we show how the longing to worship meets its fulfillment only in Christ Jesus. But when we're tempted to accommodate the culture, instead of revealing an idol, we choose to ignore or baptize it. For example, perhaps you are working to engage a culture that suffers from an idol of radical sexual autonomy. You then meet with a friend over lunch to talk about life, and the friend reveals that their life of promiscuity is leaving them empty. You take the opportunity to point out that God didn't design us to be with multiple partners and that the act of intercourse unites people as one flesh. This response opens new conversations about the truth of Christianity and the idol of promiscuity in their life. Yet you know the idolatry goes deeper. Your friend also has unbiblical views about homosexuality and a host of issues related to human sexuality. But you are afraid to address these topics because you know they're hot-button cultural issues, and you don't want to scare your friend away. So you casually avoid mentioning that marriage is between one man and one woman. You avoid addressing these topics during this lunch, and you continue avoiding them indefinitely.

Interactions like this can easily happen on a number of high-cost social topics, like idols of sexuality and gender identity, greed, or political power. It's costly to confront these idols and expose their emptiness. Doing so will strain relationships and force you to answer difficult questions about God's design for sex and marriage, for example. It would be much easier to focus on generic and already culturally denounced idols like pride, hate, and abuse.

The reality is that if you choose to confront all the idols of our culture, you'll lose opportunities in life. Doors will be closed to you. This is especially true in a surveillance age where everything we do or say is recorded and published for the world to see. Consider the story of Darcy Waldron Pinckney, a Home Depot worker who posted a vile comment on Facebook in support of the shooter who attempted to assassinate Donald Trump. Someone tracked her down, went to her work, and confronted her on video for her comments. The video was then posted for millions to see. While her comment was indefensible, the reaction shows that any of our comments can be turned into food for an angry social-media mob because of our surveillance age.[2] So when it comes time to reveal the idols of our culture, we

2. Billy Binion, "Getting a Home Depot Employee Fired for Calling for Trump's Assassination Is Still Cancel Culture," Yahoo! News, accessed December 16, 2024, https://www.yahoo.com/news/getting-home-depot-employee-fired-194802635.html.

hedge, we blunt our analysis, we smooth over our criticism, we shift our attention to the positive message of the gospel (forgiveness, redemption, grace) without discussing why we need forgiveness. This can happen to us subtly, a kind of creeping cowardice disguised as a desire to effectively win people to Christ. We believe we're being sensitive to the cultural needs of the person before us, but we're just accommodating their idol worship. We may even accommodate their idols in the name of "love," hoping that through accepting them and their idols, we might win them over to a greater Love. But Christ calls us to abandon all false idols and follow him—today.

Alternatively, we may accommodate cultural idols because of the social clout we can gain from being perceived as "not that kind of Christian." This is especially a danger on social media where clout-chasing is so tempting. By only condemning socially agreed upon sins, you gain a reputation as the Right Kind of Christian for today's world. Just as revealing the truth about cultural idols will cost you social opportunities, so being the Right Kind of Christian will gain you new social opportunities. Media outlets critical of Christianity will provide you platforms to publish. Book publishers will give you contracts. Reporters will come to you for quotes.

Finally, we may accommodate cultural idols out of shame over the Bible and its teachings. Confessionally, we might agree marriage is by design between one man and one woman. But perhaps viscerally, monogamous same-sex marriages don't feel all that immoral to us. So we feel a sense of shame about the Bible's teaching and seek to avoid it wherever possible. We don't go so far as to outright deny the teaching, but we don't advertise it either. Whether out of love, shame, fear, or lust for man's approval, any form of accommodating the idols of the age is a failure to love your neighbor and trust that God can save the lost. And in that way, it is a form of despair.

Remember, Jonah walked into wicked Nineveh warning of impending destruction if they didn't repent. And they repented (Jonah 3). We serve a God who caused an entire city to repent through the boldness of one man. Surely, we can speak with boldness about the cultural idols leading our society to destruction today. That boldness requires the virtue of hope in God's work of redemption.[3]

The Pull of Confrontation

The other error of despair we can be pulled toward is a posture of hostility and spitefulness, where we can no longer see past the idol to the person behind it. Calling this a "posture of confrontation" isn't meant to preclude confronting people with their sins in the work of apologetics. Jesus confronted people, after all. In one way or another, we all must confront people about their idols at some point. So the problem isn't with confrontation itself. I have in mind a particular *posture* of confrontation that comes from a desire of the heart.

Specifically, I'm concerned about a failure to genuinely desire and hope for repentance in people and cultures. The extreme examples are those who carry around signs condemning various sins and shouting about hell and damnation, or those who genuinely hate sinners because they're sinners. But most of us won't be tempted to go that far.

For most of us, the temptation will be to become so defensive about our faith in a hostile society that we start fighting back. If the world is going to treat us as bigots, then we might as well embrace the label and *emphasize* the socially unacceptable parts of our faith. After all, Jesus warned his disciples in John 15:18–25 that the world would hate them because it hated him. This, so the logic goes, requires a kind of militant approach to the gospel, doubling down on the offensive parts of Scripture, reveling in its offensiveness, and publicly mocking the idols of the world and those who worship them, like

3. The twin vices of hope are despair and presumption, and they are a great danger to any kind of missional work (Josef Pieper, *Faith, Hope, Love* [San Francisco, CA: Ignatius, 2012], 113). In despair you come to believe that the person(s) you are bearing witness to are damned, and so they are not worth your effort. In presumption you assume that they are already Christian or that God will save them so there is no need for you to act. The virtue of hope calls for bold action while trusting in God's perfect will.

Elijah mocking the prophets of Baal in 1 Kings 18. Any sensitivity toward your audience is viewed as accommodating. Any careful use of language or nuance is viewed as pandering. Any attempt to understand cultural context is relativism. Only the raw, unfiltered law is an acceptable form of evangelism. Our task is to confront people with their deaf, dumb, and mute idols and the disgusting ways those idols demand worship. What people need is to be shocked by the grossness of their idols, boldly confronted with the lifelessness of them, not to be understood and gracefully led to the gospel.

This posture toward cultural apologetics has a number of problems. We can see the first problem in the example I just gave: the idea that we either boldly confront idols or gracefully lead people to the gospel. This is the false dichotomy of the confrontational posture. The assumption is that you can't both boldly reveal the lifelessness of idols *and* take time to understand why people are attracted to those idols, leading them compassionately to the gospel.

Courage and boldness are required in cultural apologetics, but defensiveness isn't. And a posture of confrontation is motivated by both defensiveness to a hostile world and a nihilism about our ability, even with the Holy Spirit's work, to persuade secular people of the truth.

The second problem with this posture is that it assumes secular people are so deeply entrenched in their worldliness that appealing to them and reasoning with them won't be effective. They are lost, and the best we can hope to do is expose them to their own wickedness and share the gospel. Any use of rhetoric to carefully appeal to an audience is viewed as accommodating the gospel according to this logic. The problem here is that if you believe you can't persuade someone, you probably won't. If you don't desire that people repent and turn to God, you can't be surprised when their hearts remain hardened. If you mock them, you can't be surprised if they stop listening to you.

A posture of confrontation doesn't *invite* people to hear the good news. It invites people to be *defensive*, to shut down, to turn inward, to stop listening, stop processing, and stop considering the gospel.

This is not to imply that a proper cultural apologetic will always result in someone accepting an invitation to hear the gospel. But it will always involve a real invitation. If accommodation invites people to believe a false gospel, confrontation doesn't invite people to believe the gospel at all. Are we really revealing cultural idols if our audience isn't listening? And should we expect them to listen if we don't invite and desire for them to listen?

The third problem with the posture of confrontation is that it doesn't take into account the whole person. Contrary to this posture, we must try to understand the person's history and cultural context. They aren't less than sinners, but they also have unique hearts, motives, desires, and fears—everything that makes the idols appealing. A posture of confrontation is a hostile and alienating use of cultural apologetics that is more focused on making the Christian feel good about themselves than bringing the sinner to Christ.

Of course, the Holy Spirit can use our poor witness to bring people to Christ, whether that is the posture of accommodation or confrontation. But we're called to make good use of the time for the days are evil (Eph. 5:16). Neither accommodating nor confronting is a good use of our time. We need a different way that is more than just threading the needle between these two extremes. All downplaying of sin is unacceptable. All hatred of sinners is unacceptable. All haughty condemnations of idols, especially without the desire to see someone repent, is unacceptable.

So what's the alternative?

A Posture of Grace

To practice cultural apologetics faithfully, you must have a posture of grace, which means a desire to understand the person or culture in front of you, a desire for them to see their idols as lifeless, and a desire for them to repent and turn to Christ.

Notice the focus on *desire*. We have been discussing posture a lot in this chapter because the posture of our hearts toward the people we're witnessing to has a tremendous effect on how we do apologetics. A posture of grace involves a desire in your heart for good—good for the person or culture you are witnessing to and glorifying to God.

You begin with a desire to understand the person or culture in front of you, to know them out of love. Who are they? What is their story? What is their cultural context? What brings them joy? What makes them anxious? What are they afraid of?

Answering these questions takes time. It requires building a relationship and investing in their life, whether that is the life of an individual or a culture. For a culture, this looks like reading books (fiction and nonfiction) and important cultural thinkers, watching films, listening to music, observing trends and attitudes. With both people and cultures, it involves being with them across time and understanding their motives. The goal here isn't to act like a surgeon, carefully slicing through flesh to cut out a cancerous idol, but like a friend you are "loving in order to know," as philosopher Esther Lightcap Meek describes it.[4] As you get to know them, try to identify the most significant idols in their lives. Over time, they should reveal themselves to you, particularly in their insecurities, anxieties, and pride. And through that process of understanding will come the insight about where the idols are found. You might ask questions like these: What motivates a person or a culture? What do they worship? And maybe most importantly, why are they attracted to that idol? Certainly, sin is part of the answer, but are they also looking for approval, validation, safety, security, pleasure, or happiness? In other words, are they looking to the idol for something only God can rightly provide?

In this process of loving to know someone (whether that be an individual or a culture), we must use the virtue of prudence.[5] We see

4. Esther Lightcap Meek, *A Little Manual for Knowing* (Eugene, OR: Cascade, 2014), 18.
5. The virtue of prudence involves seeing reality accurately, deliberating on what the right action is (according to the Good as defined by God), making a decision, and then acting decisively on that decision. For more on this, see Josef Pieper, *The Four Cardinal Virtues* (repr., Notre Dame, IN: University of Notre Dame Press, 2010).

this in Christ's words in Matthew 10:16: "Behold, I am sending you out as sheep in the midst of wolves, so be wise as serpents and innocent as doves." While in context this verse is focused on persecution, it has broader application. For example, the principle that we should be "wise as serpents and innocent as doves" while we minister among wolves implies we ought to use carefully considered rhetoric.[6] As we engage in cultural apologetics, we ought to weigh our words, discerning what language will most effectively invite someone to open up to us. That's prudence or wisdom. And innocence is pursuing this knowledge out of genuine love and interest. In the case of a culture, this looks like spending time investigating artifacts, reading its history, engaging its most insightful thinkers. In general, we're to follow Paul's practice of becoming "all things to all people" (1 Cor. 9:22).

Once we have devoted time to know a person or a culture well enough to identify their most powerful idols, we should desire to reveal those idols to them. This requires courage and boldness as well as prudence. We want to help them see the emptiness of the idols themselves, that they are led by the hand to perceive they have been worshiping false gods. In my book *You Are Not Your Own*, I try to do this by honestly but boldly describing the disordered environment of the contemporary world that is based on the assumption that we are our own and belong to ourselves.[7] Ideally, the reader recognizes and feels the anxiety of this world and sees the need for an alternative way of living. The idol of belonging to themselves isn't serving them and so they naturally long for something more.

Of course, this work of leading by the hand is ultimately done by the Holy Spirit. Our duty is to be wise as serpents and invite people

6. It's true that later in this same passage Christ commands his disciples *not* to use carefully considered rhetoric but to allow the "Spirit of the Father" to speak through them (Matt. 10:20). But unlike the general principle to be "wise as serpents and innocent as doves," this command to rely completely on the supernatural power of the Holy Spirit for the words to speak to governors and judges persecuting them strikes me as particular to the time and places of the early church.
7. Alan Noble, *You Are Not Your Own: Belonging to God in an Inhuman World* (Downers Grove, IL: InterVarsity Press, 2021).

into that revelation by slowly, compassionately, but boldly exposing idols for what they are. Nothing in this process should involve hiding or minimizing sin or accommodating the gospel to worldliness. But neither should there be any haughtiness. Because you know this person or culture, and because you love them, you desire them to see how these idols are destroying them, and to know that Christ died for them. Ideally, they should see that their deepest desires when rightly ordered aren't met in these cultural idols but in Christ.

Sometimes, through the Holy Spirit's work, people can see that their desires are disordered and that the Christian vision of sexual ethics, for example, is right and true and good.[8] But other times people will be attracted to Christianity *in general*, but Christ's teaching on sexual ethics or abortion or some other culturally sensitive topic will not resonate with them. Their desires are disordered, and they don't see them as disordered. This is an important moment because the temptation will be to downplay the teaching that doesn't resonate with the person or culture just to get them in the door of the church. Or the temptation will be to nihilistically conclude they are lost and beyond saving since they aren't really ready to repent. Our task in these moments is to stay faithful to the truth, boldly reveal the cultural idol for the lifeless thing it is, proclaim Christ as the way, the truth, and the life, and allow the Holy Spirit to work (John 14:6).

Finally, we should desire for them to repent. It's not enough to spend time understanding a culture and exposing its idols. If you don't love a culture or a person enough to desire them to repent, then you have no business exposing their idols, because the entire purpose of exposing idols is to lead to repentance. We're called to "hope all things"; that is, love (1 Cor. 13:7). And in the case of cultural apologetics, we ought to hope our audience will repent of their idolatry and see the beauty and goodness of believing and trusting in Christ

8. In *City of God* (15.22) Augustine famously notes that true virtue is rightly ordered loves.

as their Savior. We hope this, even if in our work revealing idols people don't embrace Christ.

Consider Jesus's encounter with the rich young man in Mark 10. After the young man assures Jesus he has kept many of the Ten Commandments his whole life, Jesus identifies the man's deeper idol: "Jesus, looking at him, loved him, and said to him, 'You lack one thing: go, sell all that you have and give to the poor, and you will have treasure in heaven; and come, follow me.' Disheartened by the saying, he went away sorrowful, for he had great possessions" (vv. 21–22). Notice that Jesus looked at the young man with love. The act of revealing idols is an act of love, even as it is an act of boldness. In this moment, Christ's apologetic didn't bring the young man to repentance, so we shouldn't always expect our cultural apologetics to result in repentance either. Yet it's worth considering that "he went away sorrowful," suggesting deep conflict within himself. Is it possible the rich young man's sorrow eventually turned to repentance? After all, the young man only denied Christ once in Scripture. Peter denied him three times and yet was saved. Our hope is based on a God who caused an entire wicked Ninevite city to repent, miraculously. What can he not do? Our duty is to be faithful with the work of exposing the "unfruitful works of darkness" (Eph. 5:11) and sharing the good news with an ardent desire—God's desire—that none should perish "but that all should reach repentance" (2 Pet. 3:9).

Many seriously harmful temptations will affect us while practicing cultural apologetics. The praise or fear of secular people will tempt us to turn from the truth or overlook cultural idols that seem too sensitive. The hostility of a secular world will tempt us to become defensive about our faith, so that instead of inviting our neighbor to see Christ's goodness, we merely confront him with his sins and retreat into our churches. Faithful cultural apologetics requires virtue: prudence to know when to speak, justice to label idols as false, temperance to know how far to press, courage to speak hard truths, faith in God for the outcome, hope for repentance, and love of the culture (people) or person we are engaging with. It requires a posture of grace, where we "love to know" a person or culture so that we can learn where they have put false hope in lifeless idols, and then with grace we guide them to see Christ's beauty and goodness as the fulfillment of their deepest longings. This isn't work for the cowardly or the haughty. A posture of grace is bold and humble, confident and gentle, wise as serpents and innocent as doves.

5

The Missiology

Subversively Fulfilling the Social Imagination

DANIEL STRANGE

For the Christians are distinguished from other men neither by country, nor language, nor the customs which they observe. For they neither inhabit cities of their own, nor employ a peculiar form of speech, nor lead a life which is marked out by any singularity. The course of conduct which they follow has not been devised by any speculation or deliberation of inquisitive men; nor do they, like some, proclaim themselves the advocates of any merely human doctrines. But, inhabiting Greek as well as barbarian cities, according as the lot of each of them has determined, and following the customs of the natives in respect to clothing, food, and the rest of their ordinary conduct, they display to us their wonderful and confessedly striking method of life. They dwell in their own countries, but simply as sojourners. As citizens, they share in all things with others, and yet endure all things as if foreigners. Every foreign land is to them as their native country, and every land of their birth as a land of strangers. They marry, as do all [others]; they beget children; but they do not destroy their offspring. They have a common table, but not a common bed.

—EPISTLE TO DIOGNETUS, CHAPTER V[1]

It's a great quiz question: Where in the Bible does it say Christians are to be "in the world but not of the world"? Answer: It doesn't! While not canonical, this well-known aphorism is actually part of an anonymous second-century manuscript "discovered" in a Constantinople fish shop in 1436, and known today as the Epistle to Diognetus, part of the collection we call the "Apostolic Fathers."[2] What is its relevance and significance to Christians in general, and to this volume in particular? This little letter is an early example of what we today call "cultural apologetics." Replete with biblical references and allusions, Diognetus is a "word of exhortation" *(logos protreptikos)*, a letter "intended to win converts, and attract . . . people to a particular way of life."[3] Whatever cultural apologetics is, it definitely includes this letter.

Fast-forward nearly two thousand years. This chapter seeks to

1. Alexander Roberts and James Donaldson, eds., "Epistle to Diognetus" (1867), in *Ante-Nicene Christian Library* (Edinburgh: T&T Clark, 1885), https://www.earlychristianwritings.com/text/diognetus-roberts.html.
2. See Clayton N. Jefford, ed., *The Epistle to Diognetus (with the Fragment of Quadratus): Introduction, Text, and Commentary* (Oxford: Oxford University Press, 2013). See also, Robert J. Strachan, "'In the World but Not of the World': The Concept of πολιτεία in the *Epistle to Diognetus*," *Journal of the Evangelical Theological Society* 66, no. 4 (2023): 697–725.
3. David Aune, *The Westminster Dictionary of New Testament and Early Christian Literature and Rhetoric* (Louisville: Westminster John Knox, 2003), 385, quoted in Strachan, "In the World but Not of the World," 701.

describe in a biblically faithful way the relationship of Christians and the Christian faith to the cultural world around them, in particular our late-modern, "post-Christian" world. Moreover, the telos to this exercise isn't merely descriptive but has the aim of apologetic persuasion, conversion, and strengthening of discipleship. Whether one calls it a "model," a "pattern," a "framework," or a "dynamic," the term that captures this relationship and the subject of this chapter is known as "subversive fulfillment."

Now on first hearing, "subversive fulfillment" might sound a little intimidating and abstract. One might ask, as the Athenians asked of Paul, "May we know what this new teaching is that you are presenting? You are bringing some strange ideas to our ears, and we would like to know what they mean" (Acts 17:19–20).[4] However, subversive fulfillment isn't a new teaching but very much in the spirit of Diognetus—and indeed many other similar articulations, some conscious but many unconscious, throughout Christian history. What perhaps is newish about subversive fulfillment is that it originates from the world of missions and missiology. As its proponents will agree, there is a broader subtext here, a mission about mission. In our training, leading, pastoring, and cultural apologetics, missiology cannot continue to be compartmentalized, or viewed as a "speciality" for those going overseas to fulfill so-called cross-cultural vocations. Rather, the discourse of missiology must be brought to bear here in our late-modern Western context. Cultural apologetics must have a missiological mindset. In what follows I will outline the history of subversive fulfillment, its theological basis, and its responsible use.

Subversive Fulfillment's History

The notion of subversive fulfillment has gained traction in the last decade. I have used it heavily, leading to Tim Keller picking it up and

4. Unless otherwise indicated, Scripture quotes in this chapter are from the NIV.

promoting it more widely.[5] However, the term is not original to me but to the influential Dutch Reformed missiologist Hendrik Kraemer (1888–1965), who bestrode the World Missionary Conference in Tambaram, India, in 1938.[6] Strikingly, Kraemer, a prolific writer, only uses the term *subversive fulfillment* once in a little essay that served as a response to the controversy caused by his much larger monograph written in preparation for the conference and concerning the relationship between Christianity and other religions.[7] It is worth mentioning this original context before we give it our own interpretative coloring.

The title of Kraemer's essay, "Continuity or Discontinuity," gets straight to the heart of the matter. Some scholars said humankind's religious pilgrimage was one of continuity, "a preparation or a leading up to so-called consummation or fulfillment in Christ."[8] Kraemer reacts strongly. God's revelation in Jesus Christ is utterly unique and in discontinuity with all human religious reason and traditions. However, if we have to use the word *fulfillment*, then it can't mean "a perfecting of what has been before"[9] or a sense that religious experience is a "schoolmaster to Christ."[10] Rather, it must mean a "radical recasting of values, because these longings and apprehensions, when

5. See Daniel Strange, "For Their Rock Is Not as Our Rock: The Gospel as the 'Subversive Fulfillment' of the Religious Other," *Journal of the Evangelical Theological Society* 56, no. 2 (2013): 379–95; Strange, *Their Rock Is Not like Our Rock: A Theology of Religions* (Grand Rapids: Zondervan, 2014); Strange, *Plugged In: Connecting Your Faith with What You Watch, Read, and Play* (Epsom: Good Book, 2019). Keller deploys the terms in numerous articles and talks (cf. Collin Hansen, *Timothy Keller: His Spiritual and Intellectual Formation* [Grand Rapids: Zondervan. 2023], 248), for example "Lemonade on the Porch (Part 1): The Gospel in a Post-Christendom Society," Spring 2023, https://gospelinlife.com/article/gospel-in-a-post-christendom-society/.
6. For more details on Kraemer and his thought, see, Tim S. Perry, *Radical Difference: A Defence of Hendrik Kraemer's Theology of Religions* (Ontario: Wilfried Laurier, 2001).
7. The essay is Hendrik Kraemer, "Continuity or Discontinuity," in *The Authority of Faith: International Missionary Council Meeting at Tambaram, Madras*, vol. 1. (London: Oxford University Press, 1939), 5. The larger work is Hendrik Kraemer, *The Christian Message in a Non-Christian World* (London: Edinburgh House, 1938).
8. Kraemer, "Continuity or Discontinuity," 3.
9. Kraemer, "Continuity or Discontinuity," 3.
10. Kraemer, "Continuity or Discontinuity," 5.

exposed to the searching and revolutionary light of Christ appear to be blind and misdirected."[11] And so Kraemer argues,

> This apprehension of the essential "otherness" of the world of divine realities revealed in Jesus Christ from the atmosphere of religion as we know it in the history of the race, cannot be grasped merely by way of investigation and reasoning. Only an attentive study of the Bible can open the eyes to the fact that Christ, "the power of God" and "the wisdom of God" stands in contradiction to the power and wisdom of man. Perhaps in some respects it is proper to speak of contradictive or subversive fulfillment.[12]

That's it from Kraemer.[13] But it's an illuminating term. Now, transpose "subversive fulfillment" not only to religion but to culture(s). This is no sleight of hand because, seen through a biblical lens, "culture is religion externalized."[14] Moreover, apply subversive fulfillment not only to culture in general but to late-modern Western culture in particular.

This is precisely what Lesslie Newbigin did as he returned to the UK in the 1980s after nearly forty years in India, challenging the Western church to think missiologically about cross-cultural communication and faithful contextualization. Commenting on Newbigin's legacy, Mike Goheen notes how Newbigin sought to steer a path through the perennial dangers of syncretism on the one hand, and irrelevance, on the other.[15] Goheen says Newbigin was aware of Kraemer's phrase *subversive fulfillment* as an articulation of

11. Kraemer, "Continuity or Discontinuity," 3.
12. Kraemer, "Continuity or Discontinuity," 5.
13. I should note that in Kraemer's unpacking of the term, and in his theology more generally, there is a neo-orthodox tint that I would want to distance myself from somewhat.
14. Henry R. van Til, *The Calvinistic Concept of Culture* (1959; repr., Grand Rapids: Baker Academic, 2001), 200.
15. Mike Goheen, "Gospel, Culture, and Cultures: Lesslie Newbigin's Missionary Contribution," *Philosophia Reformata* 66, no. 2 (2001): 178–88.

this path.[16] As Goheen summarizes, the gospel speaks words of both grace and judgment into every culture, "God's 'yes' to creation and God's 'no' to sinful distortion must be discerned through communal dialogue in the light of Scripture."[17] He adds,

> Failure in contextualization within a particular culture takes place when either of these "words" are suppressed. When God's No, his word of judgment is not applied, syncretism will be the result. The culture is simply affirmed and the gospel is domesticated into the plausibility structure of the culture. Alternately, when God's Yes, his word of grace is not present, irrelevance will be the result. The culture is rejected, and since cultural embodiment is inevitable, the church will resort to a cultural form of the gospel from another time or place and will, thus, be irrelevant to its culture.[18]

Subversive fulfillment captures the gospel of Jesus Christ as both this "yes" and also a "no" to a culture, its "figures,"[19] stories, and social imaginaries. Subversive fulfillment evidences both continuity and discontinuity. It is both an affirmation and a rejection, both a connection and a confrontation, both a word of grace and a word of judgment. Subversive fulfillment means the gospel is both an *appeal* requiring repentance, and *appealing* in touching our deepest cultural desires. That anonymous believer who wrote to Diognetus grasped this dynamic in the second century, and we need to grasp it in the twenty-first.

One mustn't pretend subversive fulfillment is easy to describe or model in word and deed. It's something to be wrestled with,

16. Goheen notes that Newbigin's awareness of the term is indebted to Willem Visser 't Hooft in *Accommodation: True or False*, *South East Asia Journal of Theology*, 8, January 3, 1967, 5–18.
17. Goheen, "Gospel, Culture, and Cultures," 181.
18. Goheen, "Gospel, Culture, and Cultures," 182.
19. I am borrowing from Christopher Watkin here, who deploys the term *figures* to describe the elements of culture and "the way of understanding how we live in the world." See Christopher Watkin, *Biblical Critical Theory* (Grand Rapids: Zondervan, 2022), 4–10.

something to be continually gnawed away at, something that's not easily captured and domesticated. Undoubtedly, irrelevance and syncretism are easier paths of least resistance, yet they are fundamentally untrue and unfaithful configurations. Ultimately, they don't give an apology for hope to the culture(s) in which God has placed us. My challenge to those who balk at the doctrinal construction behind something like "subversive fulfillment" (for we shouldn't be too precious about the label itself) is to suggest another form of relationship between gospel and culture that is biblically faithful and so neither syncretistic nor irrelevant.

Subversive Fulfillment's Theological Basis

Subversive fulfillment isn't a superficial soundbite but rather a solid statement that can be justified exegetically and theologically. The large edifice underneath this tip of the iceberg needs some visibility.

First, we go to Luke's account of Paul's visit to Athens in Acts 17:16–32. This is an exemplary model of a subversive fulfillment cultural apologetic with the concept of idolatry as its hermeneutical key. We begin with Paul's attitude to the city, his provocation and distress as Athens is submerged in idolatry (v. 16). We end with Paul issuing the call to repentance (v. 30). Within these bookends, Paul connects with the culture he has been observing as he wanders around their objects of worship (v. 23). He calls the Athenians "very religious" (v. 22), a carefully chosen summary of a rich and complex theological anthropology.[20] Human beings are a messy mix of knowing God and ignoring him, of running to him in creaturely need and running away from him in autonomous rebellion.

On the one hand, "very religious" describes the radical difference and discontinuity between the gospel of Jesus Christ and

20. The term *deisidaimonesterous* is a *hapax legomenon*. For a detailed exposition, see Flavien Pardigon, *Paul Against the Idol: A Contextual Reading of the Areopagus Speech* (Eugene, OR: Pickwick, 2019), 130–43.

idolatrous culture. Theologians have called this the "antithesis" (to "set against"). Since Genesis 3:15, God's judicial curse is to put enmity between the "seed of the woman" and the "seed of the serpent," a dividing line described many ways in Scripture. Colossians 2:6–8 defines these two states as either being "rooted and built up in [Christ]" or captive to "hollow and deceptive philosophy, which depends on human tradition and the elemental spiritual forces of this world rather than on Christ." Paul describes the Christians in Thessalonians as those who had "turned to God from idols to serve the living and true God" (1 Thess. 1:9). In this sense, "very religious" is a denunciation.

On the other hand, however, "very religious" also describes a connection and continuity. The perpetuity of human beings as God's image bearers, together with God's common grace, prevents the full realization of the antithesis. "The Prodigal cannot altogether stifle his Master's voice."[21] There is always an apologetic "way in" for which we're thankful. In this sense, "very religious" is an affirmation.[22]

The concept of idolatry holds together these opposite perspectives. Idols and idolatry manifested culturally aren't created *ex nihilo* but refashion God's good creation. They are twisted and distorted fantastical nightmares, fashioned as responses to divine revelation in creation that reveals God. As a result, their parasitic, counterfeit, and pseudo-religious nature display both discontinuity and continuity, both a "no" and "yes." They show an apologetic that both subverts and fulfills. The gospel is a call to exchange old hopes and desires for new ones, because the new ones are the originals from which our false stories are smudges and ripped fakes.

---

21. Cornelius Van Til, *The Defense of the Faith* (Phillipsburg, NJ: P&R, 1967), 190. Quoted in Greg L. Bahnsen, *Van Til's Apologetic: Readings and Analysis*, 459.
22. I have unpacked this further in demonstrating how Jesus Christ subversively fulfills definite "magnetic points," a morphology developed by J. H. Bavinck. These magnetic points are the perennial questions with which humans wrestle and which make up our "religious consciousness": totality, norm, deliverance, destiny, and higher power. See Daniel Strange, *Making Faith Magnetic: Five Hidden Themes Our Culture Can't Stop Talking About . . . and How to Connect Them to Christ* (Epsom: Good Book, 2022).

Here is a framework for a subversive fulfillment cultural apologetic based on Acts 17:

1. Enter: Stepping into the world and listening to the story: "For as I walked around and looked carefully at your objects of worship . . ." (v. 23).
2. Explore: Searching for elements of grace and the idols attached to them: "People of Athens! I see that in every way you are very religious. For as I walked around and looked carefully at your objects of worship, I even found an altar with this inscription: TO AN UNKNOWN GOD" (v. 22–23).
3. Expose: Showing up the idols as destructive frauds: "Therefore since we are God's offspring, we should not think that the divine being is like gold or silver or stone—an image made by human design and skill" (v. 29).
4. Evangelize: Showing off the gospel of Jesus Christ as "subversive fulfillment": "So you are ignorant of the very thing you worship—and this is what I am going to proclaim to you" (v. 23).[23]

Second, and as hinted at by Kraemer himself in his invention of the term, we look at Paul's exposition in 1 Corinthians 1:18–25. The message of the cross is antithetical to the ways of the world. What we think is wise, God deems foolish and vice versa. That wooden cross, where God's wrath and mercy met, continues to be scandalous and offensive two thousand years on. Once again, the preaching of "Christ crucified" (v. 23) says a defiant and definitive "no." The gospel confronts, presenting a stumbling block, a crisis, and a call to turn around. It isn't a smooth, seamless progression.

Yet the gospel also connects. In this same passage, Paul chooses

23. Daniel Strange, *Plugged In: Connecting Your Faith to What You Watch, Read, and Play* (Epsom: Good Book, 2019), 119–20.

to draw out two very different religio-ethnic groups, Jews and Greeks, each with their own cultures, their own worldviews, social imaginaries, hopes, fears, and desires. The focal point for Jews is signs and power. For Greeks, it's wisdom. Different groups, different worlds, different desires. Why does Paul bother with this delineation? Given the "no" of the cross, Paul might have said, "Who cares about Jews, Greeks, and their culture? It doesn't matter. We preach Christ crucified, context is irrelevant." Yet Paul doesn't say this. Rather, he says, "But we preach Christ crucified: a stumbling block to Jews and foolishness to Gentiles, but to those whom God has called, both Jews and Greeks, Christ the power of God and the wisdom of God" (vv. 23–24). Here is the "yes." Here is the fulfillment.

Daringly, and speaking their language, Paul says that Christ crucified is power. Christ crucified is wisdom. Yet Christ's power and wisdom are displayed in a contradictory and subversive way from how Jews and Greeks conceived of such matters. A crucified criminal is certainly not powerful or wise according to their definitions. Yet Paul can get apologetic traction by connecting the cross with their respective cultural narratives and at the same time subvert them. In the gospel of Jesus Christ, power and wisdom are "repossessed" by God. Yet in this repossession they are transfigured and emancipated.

Subversive Fulfillment's Responsible Use

The model of subversive fulfillment is becoming more well-known within the discipline of cultural apologetics. While this is to be welcomed, like any other theological construction, it can be nuanced and developed further. Wider exposure also means it can be misunderstood and misused. Here are some concluding observations on the model.

First, while Acts 17 and 1 Corinthians 1 are perhaps the clearest expositions of subversive fulfillment, it would be a mistake to rest this entire construction on these two "proof passages" alone. As we look not only at the Bible but through the Bible, we discover that subversive fulfillment is a pattern, a rhythm, or a bass line present from Genesis to Revelation in describing the relationship between God's revelation and human cultural response. Redemptive history, the biblical plotline, and continuities and discontinuities between Old and New Testament all offer up examples and tap out a subversive fulfillment rhythm.

Second, subversive fulfillment is part of a family of similar and related descriptions and models that deserve exploring. They all offer something distinctive and can contribute theological nuance, while fundamentally being variations on the same doctrinal themes. So I could mention J. H. Bavinck's model of *possessio*,[24] Tim Keller's "active contextualization,"[25] Ted Turnau's rubric for engaging popular culture,[26] Joshua D. Chatraw's inside-out apologetic,[27] and Christopher Watkin's tool of diagonalization.[28] Such diversity in unity is to be welcomed. Every Christian will find that one explanation resonates more than another.

Third, subversive fulfillment can be "person variable" within boundaries. Our characters, experiences, temperaments, and theological weightings are different. Some of us find it easier to make the connections than deal with the confrontation. Others find the confrontation easier than the connection. We need fellow brothers and sisters within the body of Christ, locally and globally, to offer checks and balances. Are those who find connection easier in danger of an

---

24. "Christ takes the life of a people in his hands, he renews and re-established the distorted and deteriorated; he fills each thing, each word, and each practice with a new meaning and gives it a new direction. Such is neither 'adaptation' nor 'accommodation'; it is in essence the legitimate taking possession of something by him to whom all power is given in heaven and on earth." J. H. Bavinck, *An Introduction to the Science of Missions*, trans. David Hugh Freeman (Grand Rapids: Baker, 1960), 179.
25. Tim Keller, *Center Church* (Grand Rapids: Zondervan, 2012), 120.
26. Ted Turnau, *Popologetics: Popular Culture in Christian Perspective* (Phillipsburg: P&R, 2012).
27. Joshua D. Chatraw, *Telling a Better Story: How to Talk About God in a Skeptical Age* (Grand Rapids: Zondervan, 2020), 63–70.
28. Watkin, *Biblical Critical Theory*, 16–17.

unloving syncretism? Are those who favor confrontation in danger of an unloving irrelevance?

Having said this, I admit that from what I have observed in the last few years in my particular context, students and pastors appear to find the "fulfillment" emphasis both conceptually and existentially "easier" than the subversion, particularly when it comes to exposing idolatry. Here, it must be remembered that fundamentally idolatry is against God—what we might call the "vertical" aspect.[29] The point of contact isn't simply that God satisfies a need, because sinful men and women don't really know what they need. Like a patient who went to the doctor feeling a little unwell only to be told by the doctor that he has a fatal disease, we must remember that "the main thing that Christ came to do for men is to bring them escape from eternal death and to reinstate them to the favor of God. On this point, men don't know their need: they only have a vague sense of lack."[30] We must be careful not to confuse symptoms with diagnosis and people's felt needs with their fundamental need. Idolatry, for all the explanatory power it affords and the horizontal destruction it wreaks, is fundamentally against God, and this opposition needs to be exposed.[31]

Fourth, subversive fulfillment is "culturally variable." Subversive fulfillment, which can be called a model of contextualization, itself needs to be contextualized. The connection and confrontation of cultures that have historically been influenced by a Christian worldview will have different dynamics and set of challenges and opportunities than a culture without this influence. While Acts 17 is an exemplary model for cultural apologetic engagement, first-century Athens is

29. Remembering provocation of Paul in Acts 17.
30. Van Til, *An Introduction to Systematic Theology*, 206.
31. This "unmasking" has its own discipline called "elenctics." See Daniel Strange, "An Apology for *Elenctics*: The Unmasking of Sin in the Retrieval of a Theological Discipline," in *Ruined Sinners to Reclaim: Human Corruption in Historical, Biblical, Theological and Pastoral Perspective*, ed. David Gibson and Jonathan Gibson (Wheaton, IL: Crossway, 2024), 821–44.

different from its twenty-first century version. Culturally, a lot has happened during which the Christian worldview has played a formative role.

In the post-Christian context of the West, our task is to subversively fulfill a culture that is a "hegemonic cultural heresy, neither utterly alien to the faith nor a faithful continuation of it. The situation demands of Christians a subtlety and discernment perhaps unprecedented in the history of the church."[32] Being "in" but not "of" late modernity recognizes that Christian faith is being rejected and replaced using the borrowed capital and unacknowledged debt of the Christian faith.[33]

Finally, subversive fulfillment is not only concerned with our verbal communication of the gospel in our teaching, preaching, and everyday conversations. It mustn't be understood as purely an ethereal, intellectual exercise. Our embodied, located, and social nature as redeemed human beings means that we want our local churches to be subversive fulfillment communities. Moreover, alongside subversive fulfillment communication and church communities, we must add cultural construction that subversively fulfills, that builds up and out, and not merely tears down. As Tim Keller wrote, in what was to be his final article before he died,

> Subversive fulfillment is both affirming and contradicting. It challenges people, but on their own terms. And it means offering them, on gospel terms, what all human hearts rightly need—a meaning that suffering can't take away, a satisfaction not based on circumstances, a freedom that doesn't destroy love and community, an identity that doesn't elude you, crush you, or lead you to exclude others, a basis for justice that doesn't turn you into a new oppressor, a relief from shame and guilt without resorting to

32. Watkin, *Biblical Critical Theory*, 526.
33. For more on this dynamic see Watkin, *Biblical Critical Theory*, 525–27.

> relativism, and a hope that can enable you to face anything with poise, even death.[34]

This is a contemporary cultural apologetic vision to inspire and strengthen the people of God in their witness to their culture, wherever that might be, that same "wonderful and confessedly striking method of life" to which that anonymous author to Diognetus also testified all those years ago.

34. Keller, "Lemonade on the Porch."

The Goal

Healing Hard Hearts and Dark Minds

N. GRAY SUTANTO

"We have three whole days together," I told John as he registered yet another objection against Christianity. We were both invited to a destination wedding, and after hearing that I was studying theology, he wanted to take the opportunity to hear all of the potential responses to his objections against the Christian faith. "Christianity is irrational. Let's start with the Old Testament. You can't possibly believe that there was a talking snake, could you?" John and I sat down together at every meal and took long walks while discussing the topics at hand, often late into the night. At the end of the trip, John threw down the towel and said, "Okay, I admit, the responses make sense, and the idea that we're all just material beings all the way down renders problematic many of the assumptions I took for granted. But I still can't believe it."

"Well, why not?" I asked him.

He replied, "Because, if I do, then I'd have to change my life."

The Bible roots the denial of God not in ignorance, as if we lack information about him, but in the *suppression* of the truth, due to a hardened heart, leading to a darkened mind (Rom. 1:18–23, 32). We know that God exists, and because of that, we know we have fallen short of his glory and deserve his wrath. This leads us to the painful awareness of our vulnerability—naked and ashamed, we run from God, and our hearts resist the frank admission that God is a just judge over us. This means that, when it comes to apologetics, we cannot merely offer reasons for the faith. We must be attentive to the dynamic of the heart's influence on the way we reason. The goal of apologetics, therefore, must be *unmasking* to see that we have always known God but don't want God to exist.

This chapter explores the importance of understanding unbelief and apologetics in light of this biblical insight on the spiritual-cardiac roots of the intellect. I do this in two steps. First, I revisit Romans 1:18–32 in light of the observations of Johan and Herman Bavinck on this passage and highlight the affective dimensions of unbelief. Concerning the human condition, what emerges is a deep discrepancy between what one knows (the sense of divinity) and what one professes (idolatry and the denials of the divine). This discrepancy produces existential and intellectual disturbance. In the second section, I close with eight apologetic implications.[1]

1. This chapter streamlines and builds on several arguments that I have developed in recent publications. See especially N. Gray Sutanto, *A Sense of the Divine: An Affective Model of General Revelation from the Reformed Tradition* (Cambridge: Cambridge University Press, 2025); Sutanto, *God and Humanity: Herman Bavinck and Theological Anthropology* (London: T&T Clark, 2024); Sutanto, *For Us and Our Salvation: The Biblical Doctrines of Humanity and Sin* (Bellingham, WS: Lexham, 2025); Sutanto, "On Revelation and the Psychical Effects of Sin: Toward a Constructive Proposal," in *Ruined Sinners to Reclaim: Sin and Depravity in Historical, Biblical, Theological, and Pastoral Perspective*, ed. David Gibson and Jonathan Gibson (Wheaton, IL: Crossway, 2024), 669–98.

Romans 1 on Knowing and Suppressing

Paul's analysis of unbelief in Romans 1 presupposes the connection between mind and heart. Scripture often associates the heart closely with the mind, and at other times would use them interchangeably (Pss. 7:9; 64:6; 73:21; 1 Chron. 22:19; Jer. 17:10; Matt. 22:37; Phil. 4:7; Heb. 8:10). The heart refers not to the isolated emotional life of a person but to the direction and agency of the whole human being. Thus, as Proverbs 4:23 shows us, one needs to keep the heart in vigilance. The heart has its "secrets" (Ps. 44:21; 1 Cor. 14:25); it is deceitful (Jer. 17:9–10); it is the locus of God's decisive work in regeneration (Jer. 31:33; Acts 16:14). There is thus more to the self than explicit, conscious reasoning. The heart often eludes us. We're often a mystery to ourselves.

Commenting on the newer research on the "unconscious" life at the turn of the twentieth century, Herman Bavinck (1854–1921) concludes that these empirical findings on the submerged intuitions of life are particularly salient for our "doctrine of sin."[2] Indeed, "the theory of the unconscious finds support in Holy Scripture"[3] because there is more going on underneath the "space" of conscious reason, and the "mind" (or the intellectual life of the soul) is influenced by tacit "secrets" that determine its directions.

Paul is attentive to these subtle influences of the heart when he teaches us about general revelation (God's self-disclosure of God's self nonverbally through all of creation) and our sinful response toward that revelation in the form of suppression. "For although they knew God, they did not honor him as God or give thanks to him, but they became futile in their thinking, and their foolish hearts were darkened" (Rom. 1:21). While *knowing* God, creatures *suppress* the truth about God and profess denials of God. Paul's teaching displays

2. Herman Bavinck, "The Unconscious," in *Essays on Religion, Science, and Society*, ed. John Bolt, trans. Harry Boonstra and Gerrit Sheeres (Grand Rapids: Baker Academic, 2008), 197.
3. Bavinck, "The Unconscious," 197.

a deep connection between the heart and mind—as a result of the suppression of the truth, our hearts are "darkened," and our thinking is "futile" (cf. Eph. 4:18). With the help of the Bavincks, let us first observe what sort of *knowledge* is in view and then clarify the nature of the suppression about which Paul writes here.

The Implanted Knowledge of God

The knowledge Paul speaks about here in verses 20 and 21 is ever-present. The act of suppression itself on humanity's side presupposes the *actual possession* of the knowledge of God. Yet there is a distinction between the *profession* of one's beliefs and the *presence* of the knowledge of God. Humanity professes that God isn't to be honored or thanked in myriad ways. Perhaps humanity worships other idols (Acts 17) or even professes that there is no God at all (Ps. 14), yet precisely while these explicit professions are taking place, God continues to be known. It is thus possible, in Paul's mind, for one to know that God exists while denying that God exists or has particular divine attributes, and so on.

As Johan Bavinck (1895–1964) recognizes, then, when the gospel is preached to humanity, the gospel addresses directly the existential guilt and disposition to worship that the sense of the divine stirs up and brings to it the salve of forgiveness. This creational revelation from God produces a *sensus numinis* (a sense of the holy one), which then exposes that humanity stands against the *phanoresis* (manifestation) of God: "His creatures do not stand as one who no longer hears his voice."[4] In Johan's reading, then, one knows God not merely *indirectly*, "in the things that have been made" (Rom. 1:20), but *internally* as well, for God has "shown it to them" (1:19)—and we too are image bearers who reflect our creator. Indeed, God "has put eternity into man's heart" (Eccl. 3:11).

4. Johan H. Bavinck, "Het problem der anknüpfung bij Evangelieverkondiging," *Vox Theologica* 11 (1940): 110, author's translation.

If the knowledge of God can coexist with the explicit rejection of God's existence, then, it follows that this knowledge *precedes* and is not reducible to the conscious, propositional affirmations of the intellect. It was Calvin, both Bavincks argued, who recognized this "feeling of divinity" (*gevoel der Godheid*), as it was taught by Paul in Romans 1:20.[5] Calvin, after all, argued that the sense of divinity "is not a doctrine that must first be learned in school, but one which each of us is master from his mother's womb and which nature itself permits no one to forget, although many strive with every nerve to this end."[6] Herman Bavinck went on to describe this feeling of divinity as a "feeling of dependence"—a feeling that goes "underneath our reasoning and action."[7] Before all reasoning, the mind and heart already know God in the mode of feeling one's absolute dependence on the divine. Two more clarifications are in order.

First, *feeling* here doesn't refer to an emotion but an awareness that need not rise to the level of consciousness. Tacit knowledge involves a kind of awareness that informs our actions yet remains submerged in the subconscious or unconscious part of our knowledge.[8] Examples might include a submerged memory that informs our habits and that we have refused to bring into mind, or the second-nature knowledge of the jazz musician who fails to articulate which notes he was playing at the moment of improvisation, or the instinct of the infant to recognize and long for the mother's voice. Some knowledge might run alongside and beneath the level of articulated propositional awareness and explicit profession.

5. Herman Bavinck, *Magnalia Dei: Onderwijzing in de christelijke religie naar gereformeerde belijdenis* (Kampen: Kok, 1909), 36.
6. John Calvin, *Institutes of the Christian Religion*, trans. Ford L. Battles, ed. John McNeill (London: SCM, 1961), 1.3.3.
7. Bavinck, *Magnalia Dei*, 36.
8. Herman Bavinck's faculty psychology is in the backdrop here. Bavinck holds to a classical view according to which the embodied soul has two faculties: the intellect and will. However, Bavinck argues that these two faculties have *unconscious* and *conscious* levels: the intellect can know unconsciously or consciously and the will can desire unconsciously or consciously. Feelings and affects belong to the unconscious (tacit) dimensions of the intellect and will and don't refer to a third faculty. See Sutanto, *God and Humanity*, chap. 2.

The category of tacit knowledge explains how one might know God in a submerged way, while remaining adamant in profession that God doesn't exist, isn't powerful, isn't wrathful, and so on. One might thus entertain some argument but intuit that this or that conclusion must be mistaken or correct, and one comes predisposed toward certain positions not because of contemplating a prior argument. As we shall see, given the nature of suppression and original corruption, one comes predisposed towards unbelief, as one wrestles with one's own corrupted nature, and inhabits a "present evil age" (Gal. 1:4), walking in trespasses and sins (Eph. 2:1–3). This kind of knowing brings into view the notion of *affect*, about which contemporary affect theory deals. Affect theory recognizes that submerged embodied intuitions and pathways, propelled through social and embodied entrainment, informs our explicit theorizing.[9]

Second, it is a feeling, or tacit awareness, of one's dependence before God. Why dependence? Romans 1 shows that God has implanted in every person knowledge of the divine power and wrath against sin. Knowledge of divine power accentuates God as the Creator of all things and thus the one on whom creaturely life hangs. And knowledge of the wrath of God accentuates the accountability sinners have before God. Both divine power and wrath disclosed in general revelation thus bring into view the absolute vulnerability of the sinner before God. Sinners stand naked and ashamed. Ever since the fall, humans have clothed themselves with fig leaves, hiding from God, seeking to eradicate their sense of shame.

This pretheoretical, and at times unconscious, knowledge of God brings us to the nature of suppression. Precisely because we seek to eradicate our sense of our absolute vulnerability before God, we suppress the truths that God has instilled within us through creation.

9. On the theological application of affect theory, see Sutanto, *God and Humanity*, esp. chaps. 3–4; Simeon Zahl, *The Holy Spirit and Christian Experience* (Oxford: Oxford University Press, 2022).

Suppression

Suppression, for Paul, is not about inferring the wrong beliefs about God (though it might lead to that) but about ways the fallen heart holds down truth it knows of God. It is about holding down the implanted knowledge of God because the heart loves the creature over the Creator and refuses to acknowledge vulnerability before him. Suppression precedes theoretical awareness because the heart has become darkened, and the explicit profession of the mind (denying God honor and thanks) is in conflict with the deeper implanted knowledge of God. The heart (soul) directs the mind (a faculty of the soul), and because the heart loves something other than God, the mind fails to reason appropriately about God and refuses to apprehend the implanted knowledge of God.

Johan Bavinck's exegetical comments on Romans 1 are again helpful, illumining the character of suppression:

> We need to keep a sharp eye on the fact that there is something distorted in the human condition. People have been resisting, suppressing. They have done so unconsciously. But they do so all the time, moment by moment *always unaware that they are doing so.* But at the same time, there is always a definite unsettledness deep within them as a consequence of that suppression. . . . The engine of this suppressing process runs noiselessly, but not so noiselessly that they never feel it running now and then and thereby realize that something is amiss in their lives. People play hide-and-seek with God.[10]

Because humans are religious creatures always in contact with God, an existential "unsettledness" results from their suppression of the sense of the divine. Furthermore, because the sense of divinity is

10. Johan Bavinck, "Christian Faith and Religious Consciousness," in *The J. H. Bavinck Reader*, trans. J. A. De Jong, ed. J. Bolt, J. Bratt, and P. J. Visser (Grand Rapids: Eerdmans, 2013), 285. Emphasis mine.

implanted by an active work of God himself, they cannot ultimately eradicate it:

> Man has repressed the truth of the everlasting power and the divinity of God. It has been exiled to his unconscious, to the crypts of his existence. That does not mean though that it has vanished forever. Still active, it reveals itself again and again. But it cannot become openly conscious; it appears in disguise, and it is exchanged for something different.[11]

The sense of divinity pops up "in disguise" due to the heart's desire to repress the truth. It shows up in our intuitions and talk of norms, an ultimate problem concerning the world and its solution, belonging, destiny, and a higher power. (Johan calls these the magnetic points.)

An analogy might help to capture Johan's emphases here. Consider a family in which an estranged child, now an adult, receives daily texts from a sibling about their mother, who has been diagnosed with a fatal disease. Their mother has only a few more years to live. These texts beckon the child to come home, but the child has become so accustomed to living on his own and ignoring the family that he refuses to respond or read the daily text messages. After a few months, the text messages are treated no longer as minor nuisances that require conscious deleting but become ignored altogether, grouped with all of the other unread messages he receives, receding into the back of his subconscious. The child can go about his daily business without consciously thinking about the messages or his mother despite it being there in his subconscious—that is, of course, until that distant sibling shows up on his doorstep, forcing him to recall all the messages he had so successfully (in self-deception) coped with through suppression.

11. Johan Bavinck, *The Church Between the Temple and the Mosque* (Glenside, PA: Westminster Seminary Press, 2023), 117–18.

Similarly, for Johan general revelation is that visceral feeling or unconscious knowledge of God that all creatures experience by virtue of God's revealing act. One might no longer be attentive to it, but it can never be forgotten or eradicated. It manifests in ongoing idolatries and existential angst. Certain prompts—such as exposure to great beauty, a conversation about the meaning of mortality, or attending a church service where the word is preached—might cause sinners to be confronted again with this sense of the divine they have long submerged. For Johan, an isolated emphasis on propositions and arguments for God's existence as a reading of Romans 1 domesticates the force of this Pauline passage and misses its concrete teachings.

Apologetic Implications

With an affectively informed reading of Romans 1 in view, there are at least eight apologetic implications to consider.

First, apologetics isn't about moving non-Christians from ignorance to the knowledge of God but about unmasking the fact that non-Christians already know God. The problem is suppression, not ignorance. This means apologetics is a moral enterprise as much as it is intellectual; it is as much pastoral as it is philosophical.

Second, unbelief isn't primarily an intellectual problem but an affective one. Failure to acknowledge God isn't due to the lack of arguments, evidence, or awareness of the knowledge of God but due to the corruption of our hearts. We don't want God to exist, for acknowledging his existence and glory means simultaneously acknowledging our maximal vulnerability before him (Rom. 1:32). While apologetic arguments may be helpful to show that sinners are "without excuse," sinners may be motivated to suppress truth of God so they can protect their sin patterns. As we saw with John at the beginning of this chapter, intellectual objections we raise against Christian faith, while real, are motivated by the heart's resistance to God.

Third, apologetics should aim to expose the discrepancy between the sense of divinity that all have and the profession of unbelief. This gap between knowledge and profession creates an existential disturbance that apologetics exposes. This can take the shape of many forms: Perhaps it's a gap between what one asserts and how one feels—one might assert that life is meaningless, for instance, but cannot help but feel otherwise, and even manifest that feeling by arguing about great injustice in the world that must be fixed. Maybe the gap can be exposed by showing intellectual inconsistency in the unbelieving worldview; for instance, the non-Christian might argue that all morality is relative while insisting that there is a right way to conduct one's self.

Fourth, apologetics should be theologically informed and thus contextually and culturally pliable. Because the sense of the divine manifests itself under repression in different ways, the apologist should carefully listen to discern discrepancies or idolatries. Though awareness of the best apologetic arguments can be helpful (e.g., the moral, cosmological, teleological, or transcendental argument), apologetics cannot be reduced to repeating these arguments. At worst, such an approach can render the apologist incapable of listening carefully to the desires, intuitions, or idolatries of the interlocutor as the apologist is merely waiting for the opportunity to rehearse the arguments. Differing cultures and contexts disguise the sense of divinity in distinct ways. No single formal point of contact fits all cases. However, given the witness of Scripture, rest assured that the gospel always addresses an ever-present *revelational* point of contact.

This fourth point is especially important, and some concrete examples may help convey what I mean. The sense of the divine, recalling Johan's point, manifests itself in disguise and in magnetic points that attract the human heart. One of these magnetic points is a sense of problem and deliverance due to our implanted awareness of sin (as the main problem) and need for God (as the main solution).

In a Western, post-Christendom context, we may repress this awareness by replacing sin with, say, poverty and marginalization, wealth distribution and inclusion as the main solutions. But the Christian doctrine of sin argues that corruption cuts across both the rich and poor, both the marginalized and the powerful. Immorality and brokenness characterize the wealthy and the powerful, leading many to observe that the poor and marginalized need to be liberated from those who oppress them. Thus, wealth and inclusion cannot be the cure for our social ills. In a Chinese-Indonesian context, one may place the problem not in sin but in the failure to venerate one's elders, and the solution as the practice of filial piety. But our elders, too, are morally corrupt. They *depend* on the subordination and veneration of their progeny, even in the afterlife. For the solution to their ills, both the elderly and their progeny require a third party—a divine authority who will forgive.

Fifth, apologetics and evangelism cannot be sharply distinguished. In fact, they are so intertwined that one cannot be done without the other. If the genesis of failure to believe in God is moral as much as it may be intellectual—as sinners are incentivized to resist God due to their vulnerability in culpability—then from the outset apologetics must be presented with and shaped by the gospel. Exposure of culpability is painful and heart-wrenching. Only the gospel of grace can salve the fear that inhibits freely confessing one's guilt or shame before God. We're offering not merely truth that exposes us but also the forgiveness and grace we need to accept our vulnerability.

Sixth, apologetics must be attentive to the habits and social entrainment of the culture within which the apologetic confrontation takes place. Given the affective impulses that undergird our explicit reasoning, apologists should be aware that the cultures, communities, and contexts we inhabit shape what we desire, prioritize, and find attractive. It is necessary, and at times urgently so, to expose the ways the interlocutor has been conditioned by context to resist the God of the gospel in particular ways. In some contexts, the non-Christian might be trained subconsciously to associate those who assert that there is one ultimate truth with abuse and dogmatism. In these contexts, it's not enough to show why an ultimate truth is knowable, but the Christian must also show that it doesn't lead to the kinds of abuse the non-Christian may have in mind. In other contexts, exclusive loyalty to Jesus may be associated with disrespect of family tradition; it is thus important to show how loyalty to Christ may not lead to disrespect but to greater honoring of family. It is also helpful for apologists to care for the interlocutor in concrete, habitual, and embodied ways—meeting regularly, invitations to church or Bible studies, and hospitality are all in themselves apologetic acts, for they witness to the attractiveness and beauty of the Christian faith.

Seventh, apologetics is not just for professionally trained practitioners, theologians, or philosophers but for every Christian, because every Christian is called to defend the faith (1 Pet. 3:15), disciple, and evangelize. God has equipped Christians with sufficient resources to cultivate wisdom and worldview, to be sensitive to the heart's deceptions, and to illumine the mind's darkness.

Finally, apologetics is necessary not just for those who don't yet believe but also for those who believe. The human heart holds deceptive secrets, and believers must continue to be vigilant from the ways they too continue to nurture the self-defensiveness, fear, and pride that cause us to resist the exposing and sanctifying witness of the gospel. Indwelling sin continues to trouble the believer. And if apologetics unmasks the discrepancy between what one professes and what one knows deep within, then Christians need to be exposed just as much as those who don't yet believe.

Though the situation may, at first, seem grim, we find in Scripture a profound hope for apologists. As we communicate the Word of God to those who don't yet believe, God refuses to leave himself without a witness in the hearts of every person. It is exhausting to keep suppressing what we know in our heart of hearts. Jesus calls us to his rest, for his yoke is easy, and his burden is light (Matt. 11:30).

7

The Approach

Exposing Unbelief as Unlivable

GAVIN ORTLUND

In C. S. Lewis's *That Hideous Strength*, the character Mark has a profound moral experience through which he becomes awakened to transcendence.[1] In the wake of this, he looks at his entire life with fresh perspective: "[Mark] looked back on his life not with shame, but with a kind of disgust at its dreariness. . . . He was aware, without even having to think of it, that it was he himself—nothing else in the whole universe—that had chosen the dust and broken bottles, the heap of old tin cans, the dry and choking places."[2] In Lewis's book, Mark and his wife personify modernity. His beliefs and attitudes

1. Some of the material in this chapter is developed from a previous article, Gavin Ortlund, "Apologetics in an Age of Despair," The Gospel Coalition, June 23, 2023, https://www.thegospelcoalition.org/article/apologetics-age-despair/.
2. C. S. Lewis, *That Hideous Strength: A Modern Fairy-Tale for Grown-Ups* (1945; repr., New York: Scribner, 2003), 244.

represent many modern, secular people—in Lewis's context as well as our own, a few generations later.

Mark's experience of life as the "dry and choking places" provides us with an insightful window into modern people. Even if they aren't consciously aware, people all around us are starving for transcendence and meaning. They live in the dry and choking places. Thus, many of our non-Christian friends and family members and coworkers experience spiritual need in terms of dreariness more than guilt (as Mark did). What does this mean for how we do evangelism and apologetics?

In this chapter, I explore how we can commend the goodness, truth, and beauty of the gospel of Jesus Christ by drawing attention to how unbelief is ultimately unlivable. If secular assumptions are traced to their logical conclusion, they end up in the dry and choking places. I will explore three such aspects of modern life: disenchantment, meaninglessness, and loneliness. Then I will consider how the gospel equips us to expose and respond to these needs. Happily, we have good news for those in the dry and choking places—One who gives "a spring of water welling up to eternal life" (John 4:14).

Disenchantment

Throughout the modern era, traditional sources of transcendence (such as God, eternal judgment, and everlasting glory) were gradually displaced. The result is that many modern people feel a vague but poignant sense of loss. One category for describing this modern predicament is the word *disenchantment.* This term can be understood in different ways, but it often involves a sense of flatness and diminishment resulting from the loss of transcendence.[3] Charles Taylor, in his magisterial *A Secular Age*, describes this dynamic in terms of malaise

3. For more on the nature of "enchantment," see Rod Dreher, *Living in Wonder: Finding Mystery and Meaning in a Secular Age* (Grand Rapids: Zondervan, 2024), 7–17.

and uneasiness: "There is a generalized sense in our culture that with the eclipse of the transcendent, something may have been lost."[4]

Taylor argues that modern life tends to limit itself to the "immanent frame," closed off from contact with transcendent reality. For most of human history, life had a kind of fullness and awe because it had larger spiritual implications. For all the occasional brutality and ignorance of the premodern world, life still had a richness that made it worth living. In a Christian imagination, for example, life in this world isn't final, and this physical world itself *participates* in spiritual reality. It's a theater of God's glory. Yet modern people tend to look at the physical universe as more mechanical and self-contained. This change has decisive emotional implications. It's like moving from a forest into a desert. Taylor explains, "As a result of the denial of transcendence, of heroism, of deep feeling, we are left with a view of human life which is empty, cannot inspire commitment, offers nothing really worthwhile, cannot answer the craving for goals we can dedicate ourselves to."[5] Thus, in the modern world, "our actions, goals, achievements, and the like, have a lack of weight, gravity, thickness, substance."[6]

To understand the existential ramifications of disenchantment, imagine what it feels like going on a date with someone you've loved your entire life. It's exciting, adventurous, adrenal. Everything is on the line! Now imagine when you get there, a different person has shown up—a person you have no interest in. How does the date feel different? You can go through the motions but with a sense of anticlimax. The magic is gone. Or imagine the first time you really got lost in a good novel. You were captivated by the heroes and villains and the drama of the plot. It felt *important*. Now imagine instead reading a mediocre old magazine for the hundredth time. Turning the pages takes willpower. The magic is gone. We could stack up more metaphors, but hopefully the *feeling* of disenchantment is clear.

4. Charles Taylor, *A Secular Age* (Cambridge, MA: Belknap, 2007), 307.
5. Taylor, *A Secular Age*, 717.
6. Taylor, *A Secular Age*, 307.

The dreadful point is this: For modernity, *life itself* is disenchanted. It's not just the girl, not just the book; it's *everything*.

It's important to understand that most modern people aren't fully consciously aware of these dynamics. We can live and move among "the dry and choking places" while only dimly sensing that something is missing. Often it takes significant slowing down and self-reflection to come to terms with this deep sense of emptiness that pervades our lives. In *Making Sense of God*, Tim Keller argues that modern people tend to live in denial of our situation: "On the whole, we are in denial about the depth and magnitude of our discontent. . . . It usually takes years to break through and dispel the denial in order to see the magnitude and dimension of our dissatisfaction in life."[7] This means we will often need to help those around us reflect on and come to terms with the personal implications of modern disenchantment.

Meaninglessness

Modern life is also characterized by the tragic reality of meaninglessness, which is related to but distinct from disenchantment. Whereas disenchantment means the loss of magic, meaninglessness means the loss of order and purpose. Unmoored from God, human life has become characterized by a sense of chaos and disintegration. Lacking a transcendent anchor, we become free to determine who and what we are, how and why to live. But this subjective, self-constructed meaning is flimsy (for example, it often fails to sustain us during deep or traumatic suffering).

This sense of cosmic meaninglessness is at the root of Friedrich Nietzsche's famous analysis of the "death of God."[8] Nietzsche used

7. Tim Keller, *Making Sense of God: An Invitation to the Skeptical* (New York: Viking, 2016), 80.
8. Walter Kaufmann refers to the "death of God" in this passage as "an attempt at a diagnosis of contemporary civilization, not a metaphysical speculation about ultimate reality." *Nietzsche: Philosopher, Psychologist, Antichrist*, 4th ed. (Princeton, NJ: Princeton University Press, 1974), 100.

this phrase to refer to modernity's loss of belief in God. The famous lament of the "madman" (a figure usually interpreted as representing Nietzsche himself) illustrates the emotional implications of this loss:

> "Whither is God?" he cried; "I will tell you. We have killed him—you and I. All of us are his murderers. But how did we do this? How could we drink up the sea? Who gave us the sponge to wipe away the entire horizon? What were we doing when we unchained this earth from its sun? Whither is it moving now? Whither are we moving? Away from all suns? Are we not plunging continually? Backward, sideward, forward, in all directions? Is there still any up or down? Are we not straying, as through an infinite nothing? Do we not feel the breath of empty space? Has it not become colder? Is not night continually closing in on us?"[9]

The particular emotions of modern meaninglessness are powerfully conveyed by this speech and its metaphors (wiping away the horizon, unchaining the earth, plunging into empty space, and so on). Again, this is how many modern people *feel*—even though they don't always realize it.

In existential philosophy, meaninglessness is often reflected upon in relation to morality. The "new atheism," for example, is characterized by moral confidence and superiority, apparently believing it is obvious that we can retain moral meaning apart from God.[10] But this is an eccentric pattern within the tradition of atheism. Older existentialist philosophers tended to see atheism as entailing the loss of moral meaning. Jean-Paul Sartre famously rejected the efforts of earlier atheists to retain traditional morality apart from God, arguing that "the existentialist finds it extremely embarrassing that God

9. Friedrich Nietzsche, *The Gay Science*, as cited in R. J. Hollingdale, *Nietzsche: The Man and His Philosophy* (Cambridge: Cambridge University Press, 2001), 139.
10. For example, see Sam Harris, *The Moral Landscape: How Science Can Determine Human Values* (New York: Free Press, 2011), 15–16.

does not exist, for there disappears with him all possibility of finding values in an intelligible heaven."[11] Sartre approved of Dostoevsky's famous slogan "If God did not exist, everything would be permitted" and identified it as the "starting point" for existentialist thought.[12]

Similarly, for Albert Camus, atheism entailed that transcendent meaning (about morality and everything else) is ultimately unknowable and thus irrelevant to human existence: "I don't know whether this world has a meaning that transcends it. But I know that I do not know that meaning and that it is impossible for me just now to know it. What can a meaning outside my condition mean to me?"[13] Camus argued that our inherent desire for meaning in a world that has revealed itself to be ultimately meaningless results in a sense of absurdity. The only logical question is whether suicide is the appropriate response.

Again, the point isn't that modern people are constantly thinking about meaninglessness at a conscious level. I'm talking about the atmosphere in which we function (from which we are frequently distracted). Often it will only become fully evident to us if we slow down to consider larger questions of purpose and meaning. Yet the huge spike in anxiety and depression in recent years suggests that the concerns of these existentialist philosophers have not lost their relevance. And soberingly, to Camus's point, suicide rates continue to rise.[14]

Loneliness

Of the various ills of modernity, loneliness is sometimes overlooked. Compared to disenchantment and meaninglessness, it might seem

11. Jean-Paul Sartre, "Existentialism Is a Humanism," in *Existentialism from Dostoevsky to Sartre*, ed. Walter Kaufmann, rev. ed. (New York: Plume, 2004), 353.
12. Sartre, "Existentialism Is a Humanism," 353. For more on Sartre's relation to Nietzsche and Dostoevsky, see my *Why God Makes Sense in a World That Doesn't: The Beauty of Christian Theism* (Grand Rapids: Baker Academic, 2021), 130–33.
13. Albert Camus, *The Myth of Sisyphus and Other Essays* (New York: Vintage, 2012), 151.
14. Lisa Marshall, "Suicide Rates in the US Are on the Rise: New Study Offers Surprising Reasons Why," CU Boulder Today, February 15, 2024, https://www.colorado.edu/today/2024/02/15/suicide-rates-us-are-rise-new-study-offers-surprising-reasons-why.

relatively mild. Whereas those terrors are more vertical, loneliness appears as more of a mere social (horizontal) problem. But a good case can be made that loneliness is just as devastating, not least because we often fail to notice it. It's truly a silent killer.

I first came to terms with the modern problem of loneliness when I wrote my doctoral dissertation on Anselm of Canterbury (a medieval monk). In the context of my research, I spent a lot of time reading Anselm's letters. What surprised me more than anything else about his thought was his exalted doctrine of friendship. Anselm believed two friends could be spiritually united through love. He spoke of "those whose minds the fire of love welds together," such that physical separation is a source of agony.[15] At times, this notion of spiritual union was so powerful it almost sounded like the doctrine of *perichoresis*, which is used to refer to mutual indwelling or interpenetration among the persons of the Godhead. Writing to another monk, for example, Anselm wrote, "Since your soul and my soul can never bear to be absent from each other but are incessantly entwined together, nothing of ourselves is lacking to the other except that we are not present to one another physically."[16]

As it turns out, this ideal of the union of souls in the pursuit of virtue isn't unique to Anselm but goes all the way back throughout the Christian tradition, and even among some ancient pagan thinkers. Christians rooted this point biblically in passages like 1 Samuel 18:1, where "the soul of Jonathan was knit to the soul of David, and Jonathan loved him as his own soul." In general, we can say that in the ancient world, friendship was considered the highest form of love; in the modern world, we have made romantic and sexual love to be the highest form of love. Here is how C. S. Lewis described the difference in *The Four Loves*: "To the Ancients, Friendship seemed the happiest and most fully human of all the loves; the crown of life

15. *The Letters of Saint Anselm of Canterbury*, vol. 1, trans. Walter Frolich (Kalamazoo, MI: Cistercian, 1990), 84.
16. *The Letters of Saint Anselm of Canterbury*, vol. 1, 144.

and the school of virtue. The modern world, in comparison, ignores it. It is something quite marginal; not a main course in life's banquet; a diversion; something that fills up the chinks of one's time."[17]

Modern sociologists have a lot to say about how profoundly our loss of friendship afflicts us in the modern world. We live increasingly fragmented and isolated lives, and it's damaging us more than we may realize. Japan, after years of evidence indicating loneliness was contributing to mental and physical disease (and suicide), even appointed a new cabinet position in 2021 to address this problem: minister of loneliness.[18]

To summarize, the modern world is characterized by disenchantment, meaninglessness, and loneliness. We have lost the magic, the purpose, and the social situatedness that most human beings found basic to life. We live a more barren existence—yet simultaneously a more distracted and hurried one, with the result that we aren't fully aware how much happier we should be. It sneaks in here and there, through looking at the stars while camping, through listening to beautiful music, or through reading about the past.

What does this mean for our evangelism and apologetics? How might we expose the modern plight in order to share the hope of Jesus with those living in the dry and choking places?

Preaching Christ in the Dry and Choking Places

It's breathtaking to consider the significance and joy of our task as God's people living in the modern era. Our task is nothing less than to proclaim the truth of God, the gospel of Jesus Christ, that functions in the modern world like light in the darkness, food to hunger,

17. C. S. Lewis, *The Four Loves*, in *The Beloved Works of C. S. Lewis* (New York: International, 1984), 245.
18. "Japan Appoints Minister of Loneliness, Can He Solve the Loneliness Problem?," OMF United States, August 17, 2021, https://omf.org/us/japan-appoints-minister-of-loneliness-can-he-solve-the-loneliness-problem/.

a home to the lost—in short, a pathway out of the dry and choking places into rivers of life and abundance.

To see this, we must recognize that God himself is the antidote to modern secularism. Disenchantment, meaninglessness, and loneliness result fundamentally from the loss of God. The Russian writer Alexandr Solzhenitsyn famously blamed twentieth-century violence on the loss of God: "Men have forgotten God; that's why all this has happened."[19] The same is true of twenty-first-century despair: All this has happened because we have forgotten God. The entire colossal reality of modern secularism is like the prodigal son, straying off "into a far country" (Luke 15:13). Our happy calling is to speak to modern people about the Father's home—and to invite them to return.

Paul's speech in Acts 17 provides a helpful model of evangelistic communication in a context that lacks an awareness of the transcendence of God. In contrast to his other speeches to Jewish audiences, where Paul goes to Hebrew Scriptures to prove the messiahship of Jesus (e.g., Acts 13 and 15), in this speech Paul begins with the doctrines of God and creation: "The God who made the world and everything in it, being Lord of heaven and earth, does not live in temples made by man, nor is he served by human hands, as though he needed anything, since he himself gives to all mankind life and breath and everything" (17:24–25).

Those of us who have grown up familiar with Christianity may find this Pauline sentence unstartling. We must appreciate what an earth-shattering challenge it represents to pagan (and late-modern) thought. If there is a transcendent God who created all things, who is the self-sufficient source of all reality, then life and history are *not* confined to the immanent frame. On the contrary, all of life is *coram Deo*, before the face of God. Every moment is full of meaning, with

19. Alexandr Solzhenitsyn, "Men Have Forgotten God: The Templeton Address," in *In the World: Reading and Writing as a Christian*, ed. John H. Timmerman and Donald R. Hettinga (Grand Rapids: Baker, 2004), 145.

eternal implications, under the watchful eye of God. Peter Kreeft eloquently summarizes what it means to exit modern assumptions and embrace faith in God:

> It makes a total difference, a difference to absolutely every single thing in your life. It colors everything. . . . Your fundamental attitude toward all reality is wonder and humility. You are like a small child in a large house. As Tolkien said in one of his letters, "You are inside a very great story." You expect mysteries, you expect moreness: terrors to stop your heart and joys to break it. Reality is *big*. . . . In this big world there may be not only things like dragons, but even heroes.[20]

Too often Christian witness forgets to start with God. We fail to draw out these implications and help people feel all that is at stake. Too often, we preach an Acts 13 sermon to an Acts 17 audience. We speak of forgiveness to those who have long since ceased to believe in guilt. We emphasize Christ's atoning death but fail to situate it in the broader worldview context in which that glorious truth makes sense and speaks to the human heart. As John Stott explained, commenting on Paul's speeches in the book of Acts,

> Many people are rejecting our gospel today not because they perceive it to be false, but because they perceive it to be trivial. People are looking for an integrated world-view which makes sense of all their experience. We learn from Paul that we cannot preach the gospel of Jesus without the doctrine of God, or the cross without the creation, or salvation without judgment.[21]

To speak the gospel effectively in the modern world, we need

20. Peter J. Kreeft, *The Philosophy of Tolkien: The Worldview Behind the Lord of the Rings* (San Francisco: Ignatius, 2005), 33.
21. John R. W. Stott, *The Message of Acts* (Downers Grove, IL: InterVarsity, 1990), 290.

to follow Paul's example in starting with a majestic vision of God. Simply put, we must help our non-Christian friends and neighbors understand that God created them, and therefore they are morally accountable to God and need him infinitely. That is no longer a given. It must be perceived—and *felt*. This will involve patience in helping our non-Christian friends come to terms with the implications of modern secular assumptions. It will probably feel less like winning an argument and more like breaking a spell. As Lewis put it, "You and I have need of the strongest spell that can be found to wake us from the evil enchantment of worldliness which has been laid upon us for nearly a hundred years."[22]

What specifically might this look like? To provide one example, we might consider what a secular worldview means for the human longing for *justice* (one of the greatest human passions in our age—deservedly so). Have our secular friends really come to terms with what a disenchanted, meaningless, and individualistic vision of justice looks like? Stuck within the immanent frame, our innate longing for justice—and our perception that justice deeply *matters*—are explained reductively by our evolutionary psychology. We care about justice because it helps animals survive. That instinct is a survival mechanism with no reference point outside the animal kingdom to guide it, or ratify it, or care about it in the slightest. Ultimately, our sense of justice is an illusion, and our longing for justice will be disappointed.

If you press on it long enough, this is what a secular worldview delivers. This is what you end up with, stuck inside the immanent frame. Yet most secular people aren't comfortable with that implication. Taylor calls areas like these "the unquiet frontiers of modernity."[23] They represent modern beliefs that haven't yet caught up to modern ideas. In cultural apologetics, it may often be useful

22. C. S. Lewis, *The Weight of Glory* (New York: Macmillan, 1949), 31.
23. Taylor, *A Secular Age*, 711.

to draw attention to this kind of inconsistency and to gently ask our friends, *"Are you okay with this? Can you really live in the dry and choking places?"*

Happily, we then get to invite them to something better—indeed, to a hope (and a Person) that is more wonderful than their wildest dreams.

PART 3

What Questions Does Cultural Apologetics Answer?

8

Is Christianity Good?

REBECCA MCLAUGHLIN

"Why do you call me good? No one is good except God alone" (Mark 10:18). This was Jesus's response when the rich young ruler, kneeling before Jesus, asked, "Good Teacher, what must I do to inherit eternal life?" (v. 17). As a fellow Jew, the earnest young man before Jesus would have agreed that the God revealed in the Hebrew Scriptures is the dictionary definition of *good.* But many in our culture have the opposite response. Indeed, in his 2006 bestseller *The God Delusion*, New Atheist author Richard Dawkins assessed "the God of the Old Testament" and declared him "arguably the most unpleasant character in all fiction: jealous and proud of it; a petty, unjust, unforgiving control-freak; a vindictive, bloodthirsty ethnic cleanser; a misogynistic, homophobic, racist, infanticidal, genocidal, filicidal, pestilential, megalomaniacal, sadomasochistic, capriciously malevolent bully."[1]

By contrast, Dawkins recognizes Jesus as a good moral teacher. He

1. Richard Dawkins, *The God Delusion* (Boston, MA: Houghton Mifflin Harcourt, 2006), 31.

doesn't credit Jesus with divinity. In fact, he thinks Jesus would have been a fellow atheist if he had lived today. But Jesus's ethical commands, such as loving your neighbor as yourself, caring for the poor, and showing love even to those most hostile to you, strike Dawkins as quite good. Most of our neighbors would agree. If we could transport them back two thousand years and place them before Jesus, however, they may have been confronted with the same question as the rich young ruler: "Why do you call me good?" And as we will see in this chapter, if our neighbors did their homework before answering Jesus's question, they would find that Jesus gave us our most basic ethical beliefs—regardless of how we identify religiously. What's more, they would discover that without the God revealed in the Bible, the moral measuring stick we're all wielding crumbles into dust and ashes in our hands.

Why Do We Call Jesus Good?

The Jews of Jesus's day were living as a trampled racial and religious group within the mighty Roman Empire. They clung to ancient texts that claimed their God made the heavens and the earth, that he made all humans in his image, and that he alone is worthy of worship. These same texts called the Jews to care for the poor and the oppressed; to provide for widows, orphans, and refugees; and to love their neighbors as themselves. The contrast with the ethics of the Roman deities couldn't have been starker.

As British historian Tom Holland explains in *Dominion: How the Christian Revolution Remade the World*, the Greek and Roman gods "cared nothing for the poor." Nor did the classical philosophers. "The starving deserved no sympathy," Holland reports. "Beggars were best rounded up and deported. Pity risked undermining a wise man's self-control."[2] Indeed, most of the accusations Richard Dawkins makes

2. Tom Holland, *Dominion: How the Christian Revolution Remade the World* (New York: Basic, 2019), 138–39.

against "the God of the Old Testament" wouldn't have been a problem from a Roman man's point of view. Infanticide was commonplace and not seen as wrong. Unwanted babies were routinely left outside to die—or to be picked up by people who would raise them as slaves or prostitutes. Most Roman emperors were nothing if not megalomaniacs. Slaughtering their enemies was all in a day's work.

What's more, if we could go back and accuse a Roman man of misogyny, he would have been bemused. It was quite obvious to him that women were inferior to men, so naturally he acted on that basis. If we called him homophobic, he would also not have understood. For him, the question was not whether you were sleeping with someone of the same sex or the opposite, but whether you were in the active role. For a Roman man to submit sexually was extremely shameful. But a Roman man wouldn't think twice before he penetrated any of his male or female slaves. We worry about consent and the abuse of power. But as Holland puts it,

> Sex, in Rome, was above all an exercise of power. As captured cities were to the swords of the legions, so the bodies of those used sexually were to the Roman man. To be penetrated, male or female, was to be branded as inferior: to be marked as womanish, barbarian, servile. While the bodies of free-born Romans were sacrosanct, those of others were fair game. . . . Men no more hesitated to use slaves and prostitutes to relieve themselves of their sexual needs than they did to use the side of a road as a toilet.[3]

So why are we today appalled by many things the Romans saw as ethically fine? Holland has the answer: Jesus.

This answer came as a surprise to Holland himself. He started research for his history of Christianity in the West as an agnostic. But over time, he realized that the moral truths he held to be

3. Holland, *Dominion*, 99.

self-evident—like universal human value, equality of men and women, care for the poor, the inherent worth of children and infants, even the need for sexual consent—aren't self-evident at all. Rather, they are Christian beliefs that have been mainstreamed in the Western world because of the ascent of Christianity.

Is this just an accident of history? Are humans getting better at their moral reasoning with time, just like they have gotten better at technology? In today's world, could we construct the moral edifice from secular materials and make an even better building?

In *Atheist Overreach: What Atheism Cannot Deliver*, Christian Smith answers these questions by examining whether today's atheist and agnostic thinkers are giving us compelling reasons for their moral aspirations.[4] Smith quotes New Atheist authors like Sam Harris, who claims that goodness without God means promoting "happiness for the greatest number of people" and "maximiz[ing] personal and collective well-being for all humanity." He quotes Columbia University philosopher Phillip Kitcher, who declares that atheism compels us to become "responsive to the desires of the entire human population" and to work toward the "provision of equal opportunities for worthwhile lives for all."[5] But after carefully assessing the arguments behind such claims, Smith concludes that our leading secular humanists are falling short.

As Smith explains, someone who doesn't believe in a creator God who is the source and arbiter of all morality is "perfectly entitled to believe in and act to promote universal benevolence and human rights, but only as an arbitrary, subjective, personal preference—not as a rational, compelling, universally binding fact and obligation."[6] In other words, our nontheistic friends can choose to believe in the universalizing ethics of equality and love that came to us from Jesus. But those

4. Christian Smith, *Atheist Overreach: What Atheism Cannot Deliver* (Oxford: Oxford University Press, 2018).
5. Smith, *Atheist Overreach*, 15, 14.
6. Smith, *Atheist Overreach*, 49.

beliefs aren't supported by their God-free understanding of reality writ large, and they could easily have come to different conclusions.

I personally think baths are vastly preferable to showers—a point on which our aforementioned Roman man would no doubt have agreed. I sometimes argue with my shower-loving friends, advocating for the evident superiority of baths. But I know deep down that this is just a preference, shaped by my English cultural background. When my atheistic or agnostic friends declare with rightful passion that rape is wrong or genocide is evil, it is likewise just a preference, shaped by the Christian cultural background of which they may not even be aware.

Many who have a God-free understanding of the universe see science as the arbiter of universal truth. Indeed, a common objection to the universal truth claims of Christianity is that they can't be demonstrated "scientifically." But if science is our only basis for objective truth, our ethical beliefs aren't so much up in the air as down in the dirt. We are collections of atoms and molecules with no inherent worth. Human rights are, as atheist historian Yuval Noah Harari puts it, "figments of our fertile imaginations."[7] What's more, if evolution is the only story telling us who human beings are, we might more rationally conclude that might is right and rape is beneficial.

In his global bestseller *Sapiens: A Brief History of Humankind*, Harari stares this sobering reality in the face. He argues that "all modern attempts to stabilize the sociopolitical order" have to rely on one of two "unscientific methods."

> a. Take a scientific theory, and in opposition to common scientific practices, declare that it is a final and absolute truth. This was the method used by the Nazis (who claimed

7. Yuval Noah Harari, *Sapiens: A Brief History of Humankind* (New York: HarperCollins, 2015), 32.

that their racial politics were the corollaries of biological facts) and the Communists (who claimed that Marx and Lenin had divined absolute economic truths that could never be refuted).

b. Leave science out of it and live in accordance with a non-scientific absolute truth. This has been the strategy of liberal humanism, which is built on a dogmatic belief in the unique worth and rights of human beings—a doctrine that has embarrassingly little in common with the scientific study of *Homo sapiens*.[8]

Like Holland, Harari is clear about the Christian origins of our ethical beliefs. "The idea of equality is inextricably intertwined with the idea of creation," Harari notes. Commenting on the Declaration of Independence, he observes, "The Americans got the idea of equality from Christianity, which argues that every person has a divinely created soul, and that all souls are equal before God. However, if we do not believe in the Christian myths about God, creation and souls, what does it mean that all people are 'equal'?"[9]

Harari is fine with people saying, "We know that people are not equal biologically! But if we believe that we are all equal in essence, it will enable us to create a stable and prosperous society." But he reminds us that Hammurabi (the ancient king of Babylon credited with one of the oldest surviving sets of laws) could have justified his hierarchy on the same basis: "I know that superiors, commoners and slaves are not inherently different kinds of people. But if we believe that they are, it will enable us to create a stable and prosperous society."[10]

In short, if there is no God, we're left scrabbling around in the dirt for our morality. We have no ultimate grounds for defending our

8. Harari, *Sapiens*, 253.
9. Harari, *Sapiens*, 109.
10. Harari, *Sapiens*, 110.

beliefs in universal human value and equality over a different ethical system. At best, science can point us to a morality of being willing to sacrifice for our own biological group. But as atheist psychologist Steven Pinker observes, if virtue means "sacrifices that benefit one's own group in competition with other groups . . . then fascism [is] the ultimate virtuous ideology."[11]

So why do we call Jesus good? Not because his teachings measure up to our beliefs in human equality, care for the poor and weak, and the virtue of sacrificing even for those least like us, but because he is the source of those convictions. What's more, if Jesus isn't God incarnate, then the ethics we have learned from him are only subjective, arbitrary preferences. We need Jesus not just as the origin of our beliefs but as their firm foundation.

If all this is true, however, why do so many people in the West today call Christianity bad?

Why Do People Call Christianity Bad?

When I was in college twenty-five years ago, my classmates pointed to church history as evidence that Christianity was not a force for good. They cited the Crusades, Christian complicity in slavery, and religious wars in general as evidence. Today, these arguments remain, but Christian teachings about sex and gender have risen to the fore as evidence for the immorality of Christianity.

We only have space here to touch lightly on each of these concerns. I have addressed them more fully in other writings.[12] But as we do, we need to bear three things in mind: First, as we have seen, our friends and colleagues are judging Christian history on the basis of Christian ethics, whether or not they realize it; second, the persistent reality of

11. Steven Pinker, "The False Allure of Group Selection," Edge, June 18, 2012, https://www.edge.org/conversation/steven_pinker-the-false-allure-of-group-selection.
12. See chapters 4, 5, 9 and 10 of *Confronting Christianity: 12 Hard Questions for the World's Largest Religion* (Wheaton, IL: Crossway, 2019); and *The Secular Creed: Engaging 5 Contemporary Claims* (Austin, TX: The Gospel Coalition, 2021).

sin within the church doesn't discredit Christianity, because the Bible teaches us to expect it; third, if we evaluate history with the measuring stick of care for the poor, sick, weak, oppressed, and marginalized, Christianity beats any other major belief system hands down.

First, let's look at the Crusades. Jesus famously taught an ethic of enemy love and nonviolence. "You have heard that it was said, 'Love your neighbor and hate your enemy,'" Jesus declared. "But I tell you, love your enemies and pray for those who persecute you" (Matt. 5:43–44 NIV). This is a million miles away from the bloodthirsty slaughter of men, women, and children that characterized some of the Crusades and which is rightly remembered as a terrible stain on Christian history. But the common idea that hateful Western Christians launched an unprovoked attack on peaceful Eastern Muslims isn't supported by the historical evidence.[13] Islam had been expanding in the East via military conquest of previously Christian lands, and the first Crusade was a belated response by Western Christians to the cries for help from their Eastern brethren. Much of what happened during the Crusades (almost a thousand years ago) was hideously sinful, and Christians have been engaged in sinful violence since. But we need Christian ethics to diagnose this problem. Islam, the world's second largest religion, has a concept of holy war that can be leveraged to justify violence against infidels.[14] But we have only to look at the history of Communism in the twentieth century to see that atheistic ideologies can result in more bloodshed and unnecessary death than any religious belief system.[15]

13. See Thomas F. Madden, *The New Concise History of the Crusades*, rev. ed. (Oxford: Roman and Littlefield, 2006), 2– 4. The word *jihad* can mean both internal and external struggle and Muslim scholars debate the meaning of the so-called sword verses in the Qur'ān, but even on the most positive construction, the multiple calls to fight in the Qur'ān and Muhammad's own track record as a military leader draws a strong contrast with Jesus and the New Testament when it comes to violence.
14. See Madden, *Crusades*, 2–3.
15. For more on this, see "Doesn't Religion Cause Violence?," in Rebecca McLaughlin, *Confronting Christianity: 12 Hard Questions for the World's Largest Religion* (Wheaton, IL: Crossway, 2018), 75–94.

Second, if we look at the history of slavery, we will indeed find countless examples of Christian complicity in the transatlantic slave trade and the resultant horrors of slavery and segregation in the Americas. But once again, we need Christianity to diagnose race-based, chattel slavery as wrong. Jesus was born into a world in which slavery was endemic and morally unquestioned. His radical teachings about himself and his followers disrupted this. In stark contrast with how power and status worked in the Roman Empire, Jesus declared to his disciples, "Whoever would be great among you must be your servant, and whoever would be first among you must be slave of all. For even the Son of Man came not to be served but to serve, and to give his life as a ransom for many" (Mark 10:43–45). When Jesus washed his disciples' feet, he embraced a slave's role. When he died on a Roman cross, he embraced a slave's death.

The apostle Paul is sometimes miscast as an advocate for slavery. In fact, his writings undermined the institution. Paul called himself "a slave of Christ" (e.g., Rom. 1:1; Phil. 1:1), declared that there is "neither slave nor free" in Christ (e.g., Gal. 3:28; Col. 3:11), and advocated for an escaped slave to be welcomed by his erstwhile master not as a slave but as a beloved brother, just like Paul himself (Philem. 8–22). Slavery was a far more expansive category in the ancient world than in American history. It included skilled professionals who earned money and could potentially buy their way out of slavery. When Paul instructed Christian slaves to serve their masters diligently, he was not reinforcing slavery. He was encouraging Christians who lived as slaves that they, like Paul, were serving Jesus and would receive an inheritance from Jesus as a reward (Col. 3:24).

Given its ethics of equality, Christianity was highly popular with slaves. As Christianity spread through Europe, it progressively eradicated slavery. Large-scale abolitionism started in the seventh century, and the influential thirteenth-century theologian Thomas Aquinas argued that slavery is a sin—a view held by a succession of popes. This history made it all the more appalling when the transatlantic slave trade started up in the sixteenth century and Christian leaders started justifying race-based slavery—which is antithetical to Christianity. But once again, it took Christianity to get this evil institution abolished. Abolitionists like William Wilberforce in Britain and Frederick Douglass and Sojourner Truth in the United States appealed to Christian ethics to make their cases against slavery.[16]

What about the highly controversial claims the Bible makes regarding sex?

For many in the West today, the Bible's "no" to same-sex sex is evidence of Christian immorality, and the history of Christians treating people who identify as gay or lesbian hatefully is seen as the receipts. When it comes to the critique of how Christians have too often treated people who identify as LGB or T, our nonbelieving neighbors are quite right to diagnose the church's sin. Jesus calls his followers to universal love, even of those who are actively persecuting us (Matt. 5:44). There is no exclusion clause for non-Christians who engage in sexual sin. In fact, non-Christians caught up in same-sex sexual sin should be astonished by the love they receive from Christians. But they have often been targets of hatred and mockery instead.

Diagnosing the hateful treatment of people who identify as gay or lesbian as sin need not go hand-in-hand with affirming same-sex sexual relationships any more than diagnosing the sinful violence perpetrated by Christians during the Crusades goes hand-in-hand with justifying Islam. Jesus is the source both of loving our non-Christian neighbors and of taking sexual sin seriously (e.g., Matt. 5:27–28). What's more, as Holland explains, Jesus is the source of the people's moral foundations on all sides of today's debates concerning sexual ethics: "To campaign against discrimination on the grounds of gender and sexuality [depends on] large numbers of people sharing in

16. For more on Christianity and the history of slavery, see "Doesn't the Bible Condone Slavery?" in *Confronting Christianity*, 175–92.

a common assumption: that everyone possess[es] an inherent worth. The origins of this principle [lie] not in the French Revolution, nor in the Declaration of Independence, nor in the Enlightenment, but in the Bible."[17] Indeed, as historian Kyle Harper has shown, the notion of sexual consent on which so much of sexual ethics in the modern West is based was introduced into the world by Christianity.[18] If we reject Christianity, we can open up the moral door for same-sex sexual relationships. But without Christianity, we will find that door falls off its hinges, and we have no moral grounds for saying rape is wrong.

Just to be clear: I'm not equating same-sex sex to rape. As someone who has always been attracted to other women, I understand why people want to form committed, loving same-sex sexual relationships. But I am pointing out that if Christianity isn't true, then all our moral frameworks fall apart. Further, the more I've studied what the Bible says concerning sex and marriage, the more I've realized that male-female marriage is the only place for sex because it was designed from the first to picture Jesus's love for his church (Eph. 5:22–33). The deep biological differences between male and female are intrinsic to how marriage pictures the love-across-difference union between Jesus and his church. Many today think that what the Bible teaches about sexuality is a story of hate. But really it is bound up in the greatest love story ever told.

No One Is Good but Jesus Alone

At first glance, Jesus's response to the young ruler, "Why do you call me good? No one is good but God alone" looks like it fits with Richard Dawkins's view that we can separate Jesus the good moral teacher from Christianity's wild claim that he is God made flesh. In isolation, these words look like Jesus claiming that he isn't God. Of

17. Holland, *Dominion*, 494.
18. Kyle Harper, *From Shame to Sin: The Christian Transformation of Sexual Morality in Late Antiquity* (Cambridge, MA: Harvard University Press, 2013).

course, if we read on, we'll find that Jesus isn't actually denying his divinity at all. But even in these words alone, we see the hopelessness of Dawkins's desire to rescue Jesus from "the God of the Old Testament." This is the God Jesus points to as uniquely good.

So how can we reconcile Jesus's teaching on loving enemies with the times in the Old Testament when God commands his people to wipe out whole cities of their enemies? Or the times when he wipes out those of his people who rebel against him? How do these acts of violence square with Jesus's apparent ethics of nonviolence? The answer is the cross.

In the Old Testament, we see the ravages of human sin, and we see two responses from the one true Creator: judgment and mercy. God alone has the right to punish human sin because he made us humans in the first place. But this same God "so loved the world, that he gave his only Son, that whoever believes in him should not perish but have eternal life" (John 3:16). In Jesus's death, we see the final resolution of God's love and his just judgment against sin. God takes our sin upon himself in Jesus, who is fully God and fully man, and Jesus dies upon a cross to offer up the one true sacrifice for sin. This is the ultimate solution to the problem posed in the Old Testament: How can a perfectly good God live with us sinful humans?

If our non-Christian friends and neighbors turn to Jesus, they will find he is the first and best foundation for their deep beliefs in universal human rights, equality, and justice. If they turn to atheism, agnosticism, pantheism, or a spiritual-but-not-religious worldview, they must wave goodbye to any rational foundation for their ethical beliefs.

Perhaps the best answer to Jesus's question, "Why do you call me good?" is Peter's response, when Jesus asked his first disciples if they were going to stop following him: "Lord, to whom shall we go? You have the words of eternal life" (John 6:68).

9

Is Christianity Beautiful?

RACHEL GILSON

In summer 2023, I took my nine-year-old daughter to the Great Barrier Reef. I had grown up hearing how beautiful the reef is, and I was glad my daughter had the chance to see this natural marvel at such a young age. You can imagine my horror when she told me bluntly that she found the Great Barrier Reef "boring and ugly." They say that "beauty is in the eye of the beholder." But in this moment, I was sure my eye was right and hers was wrong.

Beauty is famously hard to pin down. Some say it has no objective standing, that beauty is merely the playground of preference. Yet there is a tenacity in beauty that can awaken us to something that feels more real than just the material world. Charles Taylor notes that "our actual human experience inescapably treats these meanings as objective. Moral right or wrong, great art, wonder at nature, these don't come across to us as matters of shifting taste."[1]

1. Charles Taylor, *Cosmic Connections: Poetry in the Age of Disenchantment* (Cambridge, MA: Belknap, 2024), 55–56.

While subjectivity is an element of our human experience of beauty, when we're honest, we recognize that beauty is always tugging on us to open our eyes. The nature of beauty itself helps us answer whether or not Christianity is beautiful.

Beauty as a Path to God

Beauty can find us through our senses: lovely sights, fragrant smells, enthralling melodies. But it can also find us abstractly. During my undergraduate years at Yale, I remember a conversation with a student majoring in mathematics. She teared up while explaining how gorgeous she found her discipline. Beauty finds us in acts of heroism, such as Corrie ten Boom's work to rescue Jews to safety from the Nazis. Beauty finds us in visions of justice expressed in rich language, such as found in Martin Luther King Jr.'s "I Have a Dream" speech.

What unifying features do we notice as we consider the wide variety of beauties? One feature is emotional response. Beauty arouses feelings: awe, wonder, joy, and delight spring from beauty—hope and inspiration too. But beauty can also provoke us to darker emotions: envy, jealousy, sadness, or pain. Beauty seems to be intertwined with longing.

Feelings of awe, wonder, and delight are attended by a desire to keep looking, keep listening. We're not keen to let it pass. We cannot possess a sunset, but we might decide to take its picture or paint it. Yet the longing remains. Nothing quite replicates that beautiful moment after it has slipped away. Feelings of hope and inspiration are linked to desire as well. We ache for that future; we burn with energy to bring something about. Even a beauty we do possess—like a gorgeous necklace or a perfect mountain view from our home—can still stir up longing as we wear it again, hold it again, sit in its grandeur again.

Longing has its shadow side as well, providing the backdrop for more than one of the Ten Commandments. "That beautiful apartment, spouse, or lifestyle of my neighbor ought to be *mine*," the heart whispers. Or we long to be recognized as beautiful ourselves. Narcissus's death becomes a twisted aspiration. Even our good longing for a better future for our children or community can shade into sadness. Many beautiful things will not or cannot be ours, and one response is despair.

The element of longing is our first clue that beauty is also a moral category. Beauty, exciting emotion, properly excites action, and both emotions and actions relate to morality. These actions and emotions, however, are never predetermined by the beautiful. Instead, the emotions and actions stirred by beauty reveal us, giving us opportunity for good or for evil. We're aware of different scales of moral importance. My daughter's reaction to the Great Barrier Reef, for example, is perhaps just a sign of her youth. My inability to connect with certain poems may just show that in this field I am uninitiated. A heart hardened to the beauty of the "I Have a Dream" speech, however, may signal something more troubling.

Our emotional responses to beauty reveal who we are. What we do in response to beauty is unshakably moral. Do we praise something that is praiseworthy, or do we denigrate it from a place of envy? Do we marvel at something, acknowledging our smallness and vulnerability in the face of real beauty, or do we harden our hearts, turn away from it, or even set out to destroy it? Do we reveal ourselves as thieves, grabbing the beauty for ourselves? Do we reveal ourselves as servants, putting our lives on the line so our community has a more beautiful future? Even a nonresponse to beauty, a nothingness in spirit or body, reveals something amiss. There are darker states too, where we find the ugly beautiful. Some people commit acts of terror because they see something they crave in violent power. Beauty, real beauty, takes our moral temperature. And we're all born feverish.

John Keats ended his celebrated poem "Ode on a Grecian Urn" with lines that have become justly famous:

> Beauty is truth, truth beauty,—that is all
> Ye know on earth, and all ye need to know.

While we may rightfully insist that he has gone too far, we also sense that he was onto something. While beauty inescapably includes subjective preference elements (you prefer Mozart, your friend Bach), the fact that it is also moral means it must be related to truth, if morality has any real meaning. Its stirring up of longing and its connection to truth reveal that beauty always points to God.

C. S. Lewis observes, "Most people, if they had really learned to look into their own hearts, would know that they do want, and want acutely, something that cannot be had in this world. There are all sorts of things in this world that offer to give it to you, but they never quite keep their promise. . . . If I find in myself a desire which no experience in this world can satisfy, the most probable explanation is that I was made for another world."[2] He continues, "Probably earthly pleasures were never meant to satisfy it, but only to arouse it, to suggest the real thing."[3] For Lewis, the longing of beauty and the ways moral responses spontaneously erupt when we encounter it are neon signs pointing to a beautiful and holy God. Does Christianity stand up under this scrutiny?

The Beauty of Jesus Christ

The Bible declares that Jesus Christ "is the radiance of the glory of God and the exact imprint of his nature" (Heb. 1:3) and "the image of the invisible God, the firstborn of all creation" (Col. 1:15). The claim is not that Christ is beautiful physically. You can read through all the biographies of Jesus in the Bible and find not a word describing what he looked like. The only clue we have is quite unflattering:

2. C. S. Lewis, *Mere Christianity* (New York: Touchstone, 1996), 120.
3. Lewis, *Mere Christianity*, 121.

A prophecy that Christians believe points to Jesus says, "He had no form or majesty that we should look at him, and no beauty that we should desire him" (Isa. 53:2).

So when Christians speak of Jesus being beautiful, we're talking about his moral perfection and, especially, his work of redemption. As the English theologian John Owen (1616–83) argues, "The graces of the person of Christ [are] as he is vested with the office of mediation, this spiritual eminency, comeliness, and beauty, as appointed and anointed by the Father unto the great work of bringing home all his elect unto his bosom."[4] Owen declares that Jesus's fitness to save and fullness to save reveal "a suitableness to the wants of all our souls: whereby he becomes exceedingly desirable, yea, altogether lovely."[5] When we recognize for the first time, or freshly for the thousandth time, what Jesus managed on the cross, we see him as he is: almost unspeakably beautiful.

Are we really claiming that Jesus is most beautiful in his horrific death? Why not rather point to beautiful scenes from his life, as when he wept together with Mary after the death of Lazarus, or when he gave Jairus back his daughter from the dead after stopping the blood of another daughter who had suffered for twelve years? These acts of mercy and love are truly beautiful. They tap into longing and morality, and they display the truth so elegantly. It was right for Christ to weep with his friend; that is the proper response to death's evil. It was good that Jesus used his power to bring healing and life to the vulnerable. His movements aren't just right in a propositional sense but true in a way that moves us. They are completely lovely.

And if these are beautiful, then Jesus's death is even more beautiful. Just as each aspect of his life and ministry presents us with the "beauty of holiness" (Ps. 29:2)—his justice, love, and mercy—so the cross is the place where these traits are maximally displayed. But this

4. John Owen, *Communion with the Triune God*, ed. Kelly M. Kapic and Justin Taylor (Wheaton, IL: Crossway, 2007), 145.

5. Owen, *Communion*, 149, emphasis original.

claim may still give us pause. Did Jesus's contemporaries see him bloody and gasping on an instrument of torture and sigh with delight? No, they saw it just as the Romans intended: as hideous punishment. "Jesus's suffering, considered as suffering, is not beautiful," theologian Junius Johnson writes. "What *is* beautiful are the divine properties that are revealed through his suffering and pain: humility, self-giving, love."[6] Likewise, Jonathan Edwards argued that Christ is "glorious"—a functional synonym in Edwards for *beauty*[7]—in redemption because he used his humiliation to outwit and defeat Satan; that Christ is glorious above the guilt of humankind because his death sufficiently removes it; that Christ is glorious above the corruption of humankind because he purchased our holiness; that Christ is glorious in his resurrection and ascension, demonstrating that death couldn't hold him and thereafter, couldn't hold any who belong to him.[8]

Jesus shows himself beautiful on the cross by connecting the fullest expressions of morality and longing. He exposes the truth of sin's evil, the love of God, and the victory of mercy and grace. He promises that our longing to be truly free, truly alive, and connected with God can be fulfilled through him alone.

The True Beauty of Christianity

As Jesus prepared to ascend to his Father, he said to his disciples, "All authority in heaven and on earth has been given to me. Go therefore and make disciples of all nations, baptizing them in the name of the Father and of the Son and of the Holy Spirit, teaching them to observe all that I have commanded you. And behold, I am

6. Julius Johnson, *The Father of Lights: A Theology of Beauty* (Grand Rapids: Baker Academic, 2020), 168.
7. Dane Ortlund, *Edwards on the Christian Life: Alive to the Beauty of God* (Wheaton, IL: Crossway: 2014), 18.
8. Jonathan Edwards, "Jesus Christ Glorious Exalted Above All Evil in the Work of Redemption," in *The Works of Jonathan Edwards* (Carlisle, PA: Banner of Truth Trust, 2009), 215.

with you always, to the end of the age" (Matt. 28:18–20). Jesus personally promised to be with his people as they continued the work that he began. In this theme, the apostle Paul wrote to the church of Ephesus, reminding them that they were "fellow citizens with the saints and members of the household of God, built on the foundation of the apostles and prophets, Christ Jesus himself being the cornerstone, in whom the whole structure, being joined together, grows into a holy temple in the Lord. In him you also are being built together into a dwelling place for God by the Spirit" (Eph. 2:19–22). In asking if Christianity is beautiful, one of the most important places we can look is where Jesus declared that Christianity be made manifest in the word: in his people, in his church. So Christianity must be beautiful because it is meant to be displayed in the church that was founded on and by Christ to do his beautiful work and to be the place where God himself dwells.

When God commanded Moses to build a place for him to dwell with his people who had come out of Egypt, it was physically beautiful (Ex. 35:4–39:30). Its proportions, materials, and objects were not just functional but also lovely. The same was true of Solomon's temple (1 Kings 6:2–36; 7:13–51). As God's dwelling place and the place where communion and reconciliation were to be enacted, it was right for it to be physically beautiful. Yet just as Jesus's beauty in his life, death, and resurrection was not in his outward appearance, so the beauty of the metaphorical temple—the church—is to be a beauty of life, death, and resurrection. The tabernacle and Solomon's temple were right to be physically beautiful. Likewise, the church is to be lovely in all that she does.

Whenever Christians have been and done what Jesus calls us to be and do, we have been beautiful. One glimpse into this historical truth is laid out in Larry Hurtado's *Destroyer of the Gods: Early Christian Distinctiveness in the Roman World*. Hurtado patiently lays out that Christianity was utterly different and deeply offensive; not what you think of immediately as beautiful! It did not have images, altars, or shrines. It refused to honor traditional gods. It was obsessed with reading, writing, praying, and doing good. It condemned infant exposure, gladiatorial contest, and the sexual mores that were considered right. It demanded immediate ethical adherence from its converts, who came from all ethnic groups, all classes, and both sexes. It was hated. And people flocked to it, much like Jesus himself. As Hurtado notes, "Of the numerous *new* religious movements of [the ancient Roman] era, only Christianity developed into a long-term successful one that outlived the Roman era in which it first appeared."[9] The church's way of life reflected Jesus's way of life: lifting up the lowly, doing good to the poor, rejecting violence, and pursuing holiness in sex and relationships. Just as many hated Jesus, but many saw his true beauty, so with Christianity. The practices of the church were not only good, but good in such a way as stirred up longing for God, longing for forgiveness, longing for the humanity God has made us to be to be restored. Where the church has continued in Jesus's practices, she has continued to stir up and begin to meet these longings. She has, in short, been beautiful.

The Perceived Ugliness of Christianity

What about when the church has *not* been what Jesus has called it to be? Some of my neighbors in the Boston area see Christianity as ugly—as an offensive worldview turning people into hateful hypocrites.

When Christians haven't embodied Christ's beauty, we've become ugly, and we must repent. If we look at Christian history, we see my neighbors aren't wrong to call out some of the actions they associate with Christianity as ugly.[10] They aren't wrong in that Christian people and institutions too often have rejected the beauty

9. Larry Hurtado, *Destroyer of the Gods: Early Christian Distinctiveness in the Roman World* (Waco, TX: Baylor University Press, 2016), 9.
10. For a comprehensive exploration of this topic, see John Dickson, *Bullies and Saints: An Honest Look at the Good and Evil of Christian History* (Grand Rapids: Zondervan Reflective, 2021).

of Christ and strayed into ugliness. There is no other recourse for disciples than to name and confess evil as evil, to seek forgiveness and the power of the Spirit to return to the ways of Jesus. But Christian history also demonstrates that even in the darker moments that require repentance, the church was also always seeking its own reform, using its texts to sing again the beautiful melody of Jesus. This point does not in any way excuse Christians perpetrating evil. It is simply true that Christianity, founded by and on Christ, cannot help but recoil at its own ugliness and seek the beauty of Jesus again.

What's more, in the West, the standards my secular neighbors use to call Christianity ugly are standards that were given to them by Christ himself. My neighbors' intuitions about what is beautiful morally are better than their stated beliefs about God and the world, because the gospel shaped the West down to its deep structures. Secularism is a child of the gospel, a teenager in rebellion against her mother. Yet she can't shake that she has been molded by her parent since the womb. She can't erase that her face looks so much like her mother's, though she has disfigured it willfully.

If I were to ask my secular neighbors, "Is Christianity beautiful?" their answer couldn't help but be strongly influenced by the ways secularism, a radical Christian heresy, wants to reject the Christian God but still use his stuff. But if I start with an understanding that they are more shaped by Christianity than they know, I may find a more promising path. Their deep structure of gospel heritage, for example, has gifted my neighbors with the intuition that there is something beautiful, not just good, about helping the little guy. This is why grown men tear up at the classic sports movie *Rudy*: The athletes who deserve a spot on the famed Notre Dame football team lay down their own jerseys and demand that the coach let underdog Rudy, who isn't even on scholarship, suit up for the final home game. Nothing in a mechanistic worldview where the strong deserve their rights can support finding this ending beautiful. This approach to weakness made Nietzsche sneer at Christianity.

Or to take a more chilling example, my neighbors feel a good and proper horror at rape as both evil and ugly. But a Big Story that sees nothing but evolution directing the meaningless lives of the collection of atoms known as humans cannot support this reaction. Christianity has the resources to condemn the wicked ugliness of these kinds of acts. Trained by Christ, Christianity insists that the moral disgust we feel is righteous. Our longing for a world without this ugliness will be fulfilled. A world that rejects Christ is left precisely without those resources. Instead, it will rust from the inside out and degrade, like an old car long left on cinder blocks, not having seen fuel in decades. It will grow ugly with meaninglessness, brute power, and despair, reflected in both its cultural artifacts—but more importantly, in human lives.

Beauty as Cultural Apologetic

Our neighbors long for a better world, and they often ache for the good and the true. When they see the good and true enacted in ways big and small and call it beautiful, or when they see what's good betrayed and shudder at the ugliness of that betrayal—these can be used as a path to the gospel because they are a path to God. Augustine writes, "Think, my brothers and sisters, think what his beauty is like! All these beautiful things that you see and love—he made them. If they are beautiful, what of him? If they are great, how great is he?"[11] Our neighbors have access to beauty because of God's gift of common grace. But to see behind it, to get what it has been pointing to all along, they need what theologians have called saving grace. This grace, which gives access to real beauty, comes only through the proclamation of the gospel.

By God's good design, Christianity has been specifically

11. Saint Augustine, *The Works of Saint Augustine: A Translation for the 21st Century*, vol. 18, *Expositions of the Psalms 73–98*, ed. John E. Rotelle, trans. Maria Boulding (Hyde Park, NY: New City Press, 2002), 211–12.

commissioned for just that proclamation. But to accomplish this, Christianity must become its most beautiful self, which means, more reflective of Christ. We must become more biblical, not less: more insistent on Jesus's view of money, time, sexuality, community, holiness, and everything else. This is because the gospel really does answer the heart longings of our neighbors, who were made to know and worship God, to fellowship with his people, to become agents of goodness and light. They are attracted to all kinds of beauty, all of which whisper about who God is because they were made by and for him.

Junius Johnson argues that "to find something beautiful is for that something to remind you of God."[12] He uses the language of reminder because of the "minimal natural theology" in Psalm 19 and Romans 1; these passages and more show both that we are culpably suppressing a knowledge of God and that we have a latent deep memory of him. This memory

> is the element of the familiar in every experience of the beautiful. . . . We cannot point to what it is or say exactly what it reminds us of, but it is there nevertheless. This is the fundamental and indelible memory of our Creator that each of us has. We may deny it or attempt to alter it, but we can never forget it. It is the memory that we shall see face to face in Heaven or be tormented by night and day in Hell. Our worldly experience of beauty is keyed to this, and we call beautiful that which excites this memory in us.[13]

Our neighbors are designed by God to recognize beauty and have it stir them upward. The loveliness of flowers, a symphony, and the faces of their loved ones will stir longings the world can't meet. We

12. Johnson, *Father of Lights*, 21.
13. Johnson, *Father of Lights*, 24.

want more and more and more even as we're met with the fragility, instability, and decay of these beautiful things. They cannot bear the burden of providing our souls with the endless beauty we need. They cannot, even with their real beauty, remove the stains of ugliness that infect us.

Only the beauty of Jesus will never decay, will never break, will never run out. Christianity is beautiful because and only because it points to this great Husband; the church is his bride, who by him is sanctified, washed, presented "to himself in splendor, without spot or wrinkle or any such thing, that she might be holy and without blemish" (Eph. 5:27). And he isn't yet done beautifying those who come to him. He is the same now as he was in his earthly ministry, the One who brings life from death, who sets captives free, who only ever takes in order to give. This is the beauty we invite our neighbors into when Christianity acts like Christ. Beloved, for the sake of our neighbors, let's be who we are.

10

Is Christianity True?

DEREK RISHMAWY

Last year I spent several months talking to a young man on campus at the University of California, Irvine, where I serve as the RUF minister. I'll call him Jeremy. Jeremy is a bright, driven, well-spoken, and friendly guy who had, in his own words, absolutely no background in church or framework for Christian belief. We talked about the outlines of the gospel, life, identity, the challenge of meaning, and how you need to go about constructing a sense of self that doesn't depend on your accomplishment, cash value, or any other unstable, contingent thing, since that's a recipe for pride, despair, or burnout. Essentially, we talked about idolatry.

At the end of several months of conversation, he could see how so much of Christianity promised to generate a life, an identity, a way of being that was humble, healthy, meaningful, and good. The problem was that he just couldn't bring himself to believe that God actually exists out there. What's more, he still thought he was doing okay. God wasn't a "live" option for him, or a felt need, so he didn't even want to spend time working through the arguments for the existence of God.[1] Not when he had studying to do.

More recently, I talked to another young friend of mine at the gym—I'll call him Joe—and we got around to the subject of religion. It came out that while he probably believes in the existence of a deity and that religion serves some social utility, he admitted that his day-to-day sense of reality is completely absent any consciousness of God. Joe "believes" in a way, but it doesn't influence his daily life, and thus, his approach to life was virtually indistinguishable from Jeremy's.

One more student story. I saw a woman I'll call Jane reading a book on campus, and I asked her what it was. It was a book on mindset, health, and wellness. She was a believer in the power of one's mind to determine physical well-being and "manifest" future fortunes. She was convinced of this because she had experienced radical healing of severe abdominal and organ distress through months of mindfulness practices. She had experienced the truth of these principles in a visceral way and now wanted to deepen her understanding of them.

I mention these stories as a way of entering our reflections on the relationship between cultural apologetics and truth, as well as some of the contemporary challenges we face in presenting the Christian gospel as a truth.

I want to argue for the need in our apologetics for an expansive, holistic, unified concept of truth—one that can do justice to the reality of Christ as "the way, and the truth, and the life" (John 14:6), a truth to be believed and lived and loved, a truth who holds all things together (Col. 1:17).

1. On the language of "live" option, see William James's famous essay, "The Will to Believe," in *The Will to Believe and Other Essays in Popular Philosophy* (New York: Longmans, Green, and Co, 1897), 1–31.

"It Works for Me": Climatology of Truth

Let's set the stage for our need for a consciously holistic approach to truth. I want to flag a few elements of the climate of truth we must deal with in our contemporary culture. It can be summed up in the phrase "It works for me."

"It Works": Pragmatism

Commentators have long noticed that Americans are a pragmatic people. If England is a mercantile nation of shopkeepers, Americans are their even more practical and successful children. Alexis de Tocqueville opened his second volume on *Democracy in America* with this observation: "I think that in no country in the civilized world is less attention paid to philosophy than in the United States." He went on to say that "the Americans have no school of their own."[2]

But Tocqueville's point has been inaccurate for some time, as historians note that Americans came up with a distinct and growing line of philosophical reflection across law, epistemology, the sciences, and education aptly known as "pragmatism." It's "an idea about ideas"[3] that, loosely defined, can include the notion that "a claim is true if and only if it is useful," and "if a philosophical theory does not contribute directly to social progress then it is not worth much."[4] In other words, we philosophized our anti-metaphysical and pragmatic bent.

This attitude toward truth and science has entered the bloodstream of American (and Western) thought, not just as an explicitly affirmed antitheoretical theory through the influence of folks like William James and James Dewey, but more often as a general "vibe." Most folks

2. Alexis De Tocqueville, *Democracy in America,* vol. 2, trans. Henry Reeve (New York: Appleton, 1899), 3.
3. Louis Menand, *The Metaphysical Club: A Story of Ideas in America* (New York: Farrar, Straus, and Giroux, 2001), xi.
4. Catherine Legg and Christopher Hookway, "Pragmatism," *The Stanford Encyclopedia of Philosophy*, ed. Edward N. Zalta, Summer 2021, https://plato.stanford.edu/archives/sum2021/entries/pragmatism.

haven't read William James, but if you can't quickly show someone the real-world, cash-value for their own life of whatever insight you're trying to sell, your idea may be easily dismissed.[5] Unless I see and care about what this idea does for me, its truth has no use to me.

"For Me": Subjectivism and Expressive Individualism

This isn't a uniquely American thing, or even a distinctly modern thing (though it is quite modern). Whatever is true—especially in the areas we might term the humanities—has to be true subjectively. This can take more or less relativistic forms, but especially in areas of religion, philosophy, or well-being, psychological immediacy is a key marker of "truth."

This is often the inverse of another marker of the moment, "expressive individualism,"[6] where folks tend to view a person's commitments, values, and self-definition as expressive of an inner reality, unconstrained by society or imposed from without. For something to "work for me," it has to mesh with my authentic self that I am in the process of both discovering and also creating.[7] Importantly, this subjectivity is often not just about the relativity of certain prescriptions for this or that concrete individual (Johnny has a vitamin deficiency, while Janey doesn't, so taking vitamins "works" for him and not her) but is increasingly psychologized and brought under the aegis of the therapeutic.[8] It's about the resonance of a claim with the particular consciousness of the individual, their personal sense of selfhood and well-being construed as psychological equilibrium and identity-affirmation.

---

5. Hence the dominant preference for "application-driven" and "principle-driven" sermons "everyday life" in more successful, seeker-sensitive wings of the American evangelical church landscape.
6. The original work on "expressive individualism," see Robert N. Bellah et al., *Habits of the Heart: Individualism and Commitment in American Life* (Berkeley: University of California Press, 1985).
7. On "authenticity," see the now-classic book, Charles Taylor, *A Secular Age* (Cambridge, MA: Belknap, 2007), 475.
8. Philip Rieff, *The Triumph of the Therapeutic: Uses of Faith after Freud* (New York: Harper Torchbooks, 1966).

"For Me": Galloping Pluralism

Regarding "for me," subjectivism has as its correlate an astonishing, "galloping pluralism."[9] When Charles Taylor coined that term, he was speaking of the way that in the modern period the Enlightenment's rationalist criticism of traditional religion, the Romantic reactions against it, and everything that followed created a bewildering spectrum of spiritual options. We have greater psychological consciousness of the existence of other ways of being spiritual that yield seemingly, externally functional ways of being. Your Sikh neighbor seems as happy as your Wiccan neighbor as your agnostic tech-bro neighbor who is awaiting the Singularity.

This pluralism interacts with pragmatism in weird ways. For some, it can lead in a hyperscientistic and metaphysically skeptical direction, where for a philosophically simple materialist, verificationism and evidentialism can rule their thinking: "I don't want any metaphysical mysteries handed down to me by priests; I need replicable studies in labs before I bank on anything." For others, ironically enough, it can lead in an opposing direction: "I don't need a bunch of funded lab studies, handed down from the medical establishment; I have tested and experienced the power of healing crystals myself and know it to be true."[10] When you add in the wild west of the internet and the algorithm, you can imagine there are a million more or less coherent combinations down the line from these, and the variety

9. Taylor, *A Secular Age*, 300.
10. This isn't a perversion of an originally more scientific and hard-nosed pragmatism. William James himself was an avid believer in the "spiritual" and defended divergent medical practices such as osteopathy, mind-cure, and hypnotism and experimented to test psychics and so forth in order to prove the existence of the "panpsychic realm." Menand, *The Metaphysical Club*, 90–91. Indeed, the birth of the spiritualist movements in the nineteenth century has always had overlapping origins with the birth and practice of modern science, on which, see Dominic Green, *The Religious Revolution: The Birth of Modern Spirituality, 1848–1898* (New York: Farrar, Strauss and Giroux, 2022). Arguably, the impulse to find a unified field of the natural and supernatural order in a deeper, spiritual self has been there far longer. Michael Horton, *Shaman and Sage: The Roots of "Spiritual but Not Religious" in Antiquity*, vol. 1, *The Divine Self* (Grand Rapids: Eerdmans, 2024).

only seems to grow by the hour.[11] Correspondingly, we can see a variety of different ways that what works "for me" might not work "for you." Because you are a different person with an intrinsically unique spiritual makeup, with different understandings of spiritual reality.

Cynicism

I'll add one more trend that you can sense in the sentence "It works for me," if you hear it uttered with a shrug and a sigh. It's an exhausted cynicism.

German-Korean philosopher Byung-Chul Han has recently written about a "crisis of narration."[12] Philosophers and sociologists for a while now have been talking about the importance of narratives and stories for our self-understanding and grasp on reality. Consider big stories about the world (Christianity, Islam, Marxism), midrange stories about the nation or the world (founding of America in 1776 or 1619, liberalism, nationalism, and so on), and even personal stories. Han argues that everybody talking about stories or the importance of "narration" is a sign that narration is "dead."[13] People who explain jokes have an overtheorized and tenuous relation to humor. Indeed, it's worse—instead of storytelling we have "story-selling," which serves to "instrumentalize and commercial narration," turning it into a "communication technology" meant to sell you on a product.[14]

And so many have concluded that the best you can do when it comes to ultimate truth is find something that "works for me."

11. To quote yet another Transcendentalist, "Do I contradict myself? / Very well then I contradict myself, / (I am large, I contain multitudes)." Walt Whitman, "Song of Myself," in *Leaves of Grass*, final "Death-Bed" ed. (Philadelphia: McKay, 1892), 51.
12. Byung-Chul Han, *The Crisis of Narration*, trans. Daniel B. Steuer (Cambridge: Polity, 2024). In some ways, Han is presenting an update on Jean-Francois Lyotard's famous definition of the postmodern condition as "incredulity toward metanarratives." Lyotard, *The Postmodern Condition: A Report on Knowledge*, trans. Geoff Bennington and Brian Massumi (Minneapolis: Minnesota University Press, 1984), xxiii–xxiv. But it's needed, given the very different social conditions that the advent of the screen, the smartphone, and social media have wrought in their wake.
13. Han, *Crisis*, vii.
14. Han, *Crisis*, 66.

Or they believe with a passion that barely conceals their underlying sense of bad faith. For example, when it comes to politics, everybody knows that our sources of truth are balkanized and that the other side's are corrupt—they're being sold. But in our honest moments, we suspect that maybe, just maybe, we might be too.[15]

All of this is at play when we're inviting folks to consider the truth claims of the gospel. This is part of the cultural air we and our hearers breathe, the atmosphere in which our proclamation is heard.

What If Christianity Just "Works"?

Where does all of this leave us? Some might wonder if this more fragilized, cross-pressured, pluralistic environment might create an opening for Christianity.[16] If everybody's just figuring out what "works" for them, and a skeptical undercurrent undermines secular scientism as well as every other vaunted spiritual alternative, then Christians might think it's a golden opportunity to become unburdened by pressing the claim of truth. Instead, can we just invite folks to see if Christianity "works" for them and not worry about proving its truth? We could, for example, point to the vast amount of hard data coming out about the social utility of religion and Christianity in terms of psychological and social well-being: better mental health rates, marriage and divorce rates, social cohesiveness, measurable sense of personal meaning and purpose, and so on.[17]

At a social level, we can point to the historic advances in the

15. Cyberbalkanization is a much-discussed phenomenon that deserves analysis from material and social perspectives. Theologically, it can be seen as a further post-Babelic fragmentation, a confusion of tongues, languages, and spiritual confessions.

16. I take the terms *cross-pressured* and *fragilized* from Taylor. The first term describes the condition of tension from experiencing overlapping forces exerted upon the self as it believes (or disbelieves). The latter refers to the condition of belief itself—the way it is held by folks in that cross-pressured position. Taylor, *A Secular Age*, 302, 531.

17. On which, see chapter 1 of Rebecca McLaughlin, *Confronting Christianity: 12 Hard Questions for the World's Largest Religion* (Wheaton, IL: Crossway, 2019). McLaughlin has gathered a good deal of that sort of material, though, without deploying it in the quasi-pragmatic mode I am discussing here.

rights of women, minorities, the unborn, and various historically victimized groups largely due to the unprecedented influence Christianity had in asserting the unique dignity and worth of the individual. Indeed, many secular thinkers have begun to show an interest in maintaining at least a form of "cultural Christianity" in the face of the onslaught of radicalizing, post-Christian ideologies that are corrosive of the various social goods we have come to prize in the West.[18]

Again, there is something right about this approach, as far as it goes. But my concern arises if it goes no further. The presentation of Christianity as good and useful, even beautiful, can be a proper avenue toward leading someone to grasping its truth. But it must eventually get to Christianity as the whole truth.

The Truth, the Whole Truth, and Nothing but the Truth

Let's return to Jesus's claim to be "the way, the truth, and the life." What does it mean for him to be the truth? As the only one through whom one can come to the Father, he himself is the route to knowledge of and union with the source of all reality itself. In this he claims to be Truth in person, which is core to our grasping the holism of the truth of Christianity.[19]

In the first and most pedestrian sense, Jesus—the living, breathing, born, died, and rose again concrete individual—is true as a fact of history. But we must grasp that this objectivity is precisely the basis upon which it can become subjectively, personally,

18. See, for example, Andy Bannister, "When Your Neighbor Accepts Christianity as Good (but Not True)," The Gospel Coalition, August 26, 2024, https://www.thegospelcoalition.org/article/christianity-good-not-true/.

19. I am not giving a full-bore biblical theology of truth in this chapter. For more, see Roger Nicole, "The Biblical Concept of Truth," in *Scripture and Truth*, ed. D. A. Carson and John D. Woodbridge (Grand Rapids: Zondervan, 1983), 287–98. For extended reflection on Jesus as the Truth in the Gospel of John, see Andrew T. Lincoln, *Truth on Trial: The Lawsuit Motif in the Fourth Gospel* (Peabody, MA: Hendrickson, 2000).

internally true for me. Because he is the resurrected Lord of all of reality, everyone and in every place, he can speak to me, address me, claim my allegiance that he impinges upon my subjective, personal reality. The apostle Paul put it this way: "I have been crucified with Christ. It is no longer I who live, but Christ who lives in me. And the life I now live in the flesh I live by faith in the Son of God, who loved me and gave himself for me" (Gal. 2:20). Paul's vision and understanding of the reality of Christ's objective, external self-substitution upon his behalf has transformed and reinterpreted his internal reality.

Or again, with the resurrection, Paul argues with the Corinthians that their entire hope, their self-understanding as a people who have been set free from guilt, who have been reconciled to their maker, who have been given a meaning that death itself cannot eradicate, entirely depends on the bodily death and resurrection of Christ: "If Christ has not been raised, your faith is futile and you are still in your sins. . . . If in Christ we have hope in this life only, we are of all people most to be pitied" (1 Cor. 15:17, 19). Paul cuts off any idea of affirming the resurrection as a hopeful metaphor, a purely internal reality, a story you're better off believing even if it never happened.[20]

Christianity works for me because it connects me with reality that is true beyond me. In other words, Jesus is the way and the life precisely and only as he is the truth. Believing and living out Christianity as good works with social benefits effects only insofar as it accords with the nature of the way things are for you and me and everybody else. Affirming inviolable human rights and dignity

20. In other words, it's never a bad idea to have a good thumbnail argument for the historicity of the resurrection at your intellectual fingertips. The massive work here is N. T. Wright, *The Resurrection of the Son of God* (Minneapolis: Fortress, 2003). More briefly, the first chapter of Timothy Keller's *Hope in Times of Fear: The Resurrection and the Meaning of Easter* (New York: Viking, 2021), 1–21, makes an excellent, compressed historical case for the resurrection before moving on to its existential and cosmic implications. Honestly, the whole book is a master class of doing exactly what I am arguing we need to do here.

as inherent within individuals can only act as a check and bulwark against atrocity if we believe them to be more than a useful story we tell ourselves.[21] If we merely act "as if" that were the case, we undermine the doctrine's efficacy in shaping our social behavior. Nobody wants to live and die, sacrifice or kill, for something they know deep down to be a "useful fiction." Even if your belief is a bet, a gamble, you're gambling on a real payoff.

Furthermore, affirming Jesus as the truth reorders our understanding of what "works." Jesus's life and death give us a cross-and-resurrection-shaped life that inevitably cuts across our contemporary, therapeutic, expressive-individualist criteria for subjective truth. Yes, Jesus "works" in that he gives us a life that is truly life, but not without a death and resurrection (and thereby transformation) of your understanding of that true life. It's a truer, deeper life—sacrifice, generosity, self-giving, enduring scorn, persecution, hungering for righteousness—that only "works" if Jesus got up from the dead.

Danish philosopher Søren Kierkegaard has a justly famous passage early on in his *Journals* that gets at much of what we've been saying so far:

> What I really need is to be clear about what I am to do, not what I must know, except in the way knowledge must precede all action. It is a question of understanding my own destiny, of seeing what the Deity really wants me to do; the thing is to find a truth which is truth for me, to find the idea for which I am willing to live and die. . . . What use would it be for me to be able to propound the meaning of Christianity, to be able to explain

21. On which, see my engagement with the debate between Tom Holland and Jordan Peterson on Yuval Harari's claims that human rights are just a story we tell ourselves with no basis in reality. Derek Rishmawy, "Is There a 'There' There? Peterson, Harari, and Holland on Human Rights," The Gospel Coalition, February 9, 2024, https://www.thegospelcoalition.org/article/peterson-harari-holland/.

> many separate facts—if it had no deeper meaning for myself and for my life?[22]

Kierkegaard isn't espousing here a relativistic subjectivism or a radical, self-creational expressivism. He is expressing a longing, a thirst for precisely what Paul is getting on about and what Jesus is presenting in his own person. What he needs—what so many are searching for—isn't Christianity purely as an abstraction out there in the realm of ideas, but an encounter with the concrete person of Christ, the sovereign, loving Lord whose death and resurrection generates not only truths to be affirmed but also a corresponding way, a life that is truly life—a him for whom one could live and die, because he has lived and died for you first.

And make no bones about it, this is an exclusive claim. Jesus is the way, the truth, and the life as he is the One whose death and resurrection have rendered the whole universe a different kind of cosmos. You and I and everyone in the world now live in a reality in which one man died, got back up again, and then ascended to be the universal Lord of all things.

Finally, consider Christ as the One who is called "Faithful and True" (Rev. 19:11). Jesus is true in every sense including this one: He is dependable and faithful. He keeps his own word—for you and me. When he encounters Nathaniel, who is skeptical anything good can come from Nazareth, he invites him to "come and see"—behold the consistency, goodness, beauty, and truth of his words with his life. Come recognize in him the One whose story isn't a smooth-tongued pitch or a hustle to sell you but the one in whose mouth was no deceit (1 Pet. 2:22), as he himself was sold on our behalf (Matt. 26:15), to be given up as a ransom price for many (Mark 10:45).

In all this, I could only touch on the surface of what it means

22. Søren Kierkegaard, *Kierkegaard's Journals and Notebooks*, vol. 1, *Journals AA–DD*, ed. Niels Jørgen Cappelørn et al. (Princeton, NJ: Princeton University Press, 2007), journal AA:12, entry for 1 Aug. 1835, 19.

to present Jesus as the truth, the whole truth, and nothing but the truth—the truest Truth. Yet I think this begins to give us a sense of the holistic vision of the truth that needs to be at play in our apologetics on behalf of Christianity in our age.

Face-to-Face with the Truth

Presenting Jesus as the whole Truth—the truth that is the way and the life—the concrete personal reality at the center of the universe, isn't a gimmick, a technique, or a surefire trick to secure belief or conversion. No, it's a way of ensuring that people are confronted with the fullness of what they are being asked to trust in—not Jesus as an idea but as a living Lord.

A while back I had a conversation with a friend who used to be a Christian—someone in the middle of spiritual transitions who still wrestles with the goodness and truth of what he used to confess. He had fallen into the habit of reducing it all to some sort of metaphor, a series of stories or doctrines that encode some behavior that is functionally useful for living well. We got around to the resurrection, and he tried to demythologize it into a helpful doctrine that leads to us affirming the goodness of the body. This was of particular importance and salience to him as a trainer and therapist who spends his life trying to help physically rehabilitate folks from injury and pain.

At this point, I pressed him. "Okay, I am glad you see the positive corollary of the resurrection of Jesus. I am glad you want to affirm the goodness of the body—but do you not see how much stronger of a position you're in to do that if God actually affirmed and resurrected Christ's particular body, guaranteeing you a hope for the same?" Feeling bold, I pressed a bit further. "And might it not be the case that your hesitance to affirm that is your hesitance about what it means for Jesus's resurrected lordship of your own life?"

He was a good sport about it and took the question well. But our call had to be cut short. At the end, much like the philosophers at the Areopagus (Acts 17), he said he'd like to think more on these things.

For every person, the pursuit of truth eventually leads down the path of Pilate or the path of Thomas. The path of Pilate asks, "What is truth?" but only entertains answers that serve the self. The path of Thomas may pass through the ups and downs of doubt. But in the end, it descends to the feet of the risen Christ. "My Lord and my God" (John 20:28). Jesus accepts no other testimony. "For this purpose I was born and for this purpose I have come into the world—to bear witness to the truth. Everyone who is of the truth listens to my voice" (John 18:37).

PART 4

Where Does Cultural Apologetics Happen?

11

The Church

A Witness to the World

BOB THUNE

How is it possible that the gospel should be credible, that people should come to believe that the power which has the last word in human affairs is represented by a man hanging on a cross? I am suggesting that the only answer, the only hermeneutic of the gospel, is a congregation of men and women who believe it and live like it. . . . Evangelistic campaigns, distribution of Bibles and Christian literature, conferences, and even books such as this one . . . are all secondary, and they have power to accomplish their purpose only as they are rooted in and lead back to a believing community.

Jesus did not write a book but formed a community. . . . Insofar as it is true to its calling, [this community] becomes the place where men and women and children find that the gospel gives them the framework of understanding, the "lenses" through which they are able to understand and cope with the world.[1]

—LESSLIE NEWBIGIN

We tend to think of apologetics as something the church does. We defend the Christian faith; we proclaim the truth; we catechize our children; we tell the better story of the gospel. But Lesslie Newbigin reminds us that an apologetic is also something the church *is*. Our very existence tells a story. A congregation of men and women who believe the gospel provides a hermeneutic—an interpretive lens—through which people come to understand the message and mission of Jesus.

When I first read Newbigin's words, they struck me as intuitively true—and also as foreign to my experience.

During my formative years in American Christianity, content was king. What mattered was communicating the message of Jesus. The gospel was good news to be shared (often with the aid of a tract or illustration). The desired response was for the hearer to believe—to trust in Jesus as Savior and Lord. Evangelism was practiced by individuals, toward other individuals. The church was mostly extraneous to the process.

The gaps in this approach started to become evident to me after college, when I served in campus ministry. I spent four years evangelizing and discipling fraternity men at a flagship public university in Texas. My colleagues and I launched Bible studies in fraternity houses throughout campus; we hosted a weekly large-group gathering at a sorority. We regularly saw students respond to the message of

1. Lesslie Newbigin, *The Gospel in a Pluralist Society* (Grand Rapids: Eerdmans, 1989), 227.

the gospel and profess faith in Christ. But what we failed to do was to involve these young believers in the worshiping life of a local church.

Unsurprisingly, their newfound faith rarely developed into mature discipleship. By God's grace, some of them are still following Christ today. But it's almost always because they found their way into a church.[2] My own ministry proved the truth of Newbigin's claim: The church is "the only hermeneutic of the gospel." People need to hear the gospel, but they also need to see a community of men and women who believe it and live like it.

That's the burden of this chapter. We want to understand how the church itself tells a story.

I want my church to be telling the story of the gospel—not just with words but with our life together. I hope you want that for your church too. When we embrace the truth that "the last word in human affairs is represented by a man hanging on a cross," it changes how we see the world. Life, death, meaning, relationships, work, rest, sex, money, politics, economics, education, social reform—all these areas (and a thousand more) are reinterpreted in light of the life, death, and resurrection of Jesus.

This work happens in the church and through the church. Let's first consider how it happens, and then how we can help it happen more faithfully and strategically.

How We See: The Church as a Culture

The first thing we must understand is that every church, explicitly or implicitly, is giving people a set of "lenses." It's teaching people how to see.

It's obvious that the church does this work through its preaching. After all, Jesus spoke of opening blind eyes: "I came into this

2. Jim Davis and Michael Graham, with Ryan P. Burge, *The Great Dechurching: Who's Leaving, Why Are They Going, and What Will It Take to Bring Them Back?* (Grand Rapids: Zondervan Reflective, 2023), 25–28.

world, that those who do not see may see" (John 9:39). Centuries earlier, Isaiah prophesied, "In that day the deaf shall hear the words of a book, and out of their gloom and darkness the eyes of the blind shall see" (Isa. 29:18). The ministry of the gospel brings people from darkness to light and from blindness to sight.

What's less evident, but equally important, is that a church also makes disciples through its culture. "More is caught than taught," as the old adage goes. You begin to sense a church's culture as soon as you walk in the door. You feel it even more when you interact with its people or participate in its worship service. You pick up an implicit, intangible sense of what matters here, what's valued here, what's normal here.

The eminent sociologist James Davison Hunter defines culture as "a normative order by which we comprehend others, the larger world, and ourselves . . . [with] a life independent of individual mind, feeling, and will."[3] Lesslie Newbigin explains culture as "human behavior in its corporate aspect."[4] And Andy Crouch summarizes it as "the activity of making meaning."[5]

What all these definitions have in common is the idea that human beings generate something together. We form words, sentences, and languages. We make food, music, and art. We build fences, roads, and cities. We cultivate gardens, parks, and farms. "We don't make culture," Crouch writes, "we make omelets. We tell stories. We build hospitals. We pass laws. These specific products of cultivating and creating . . . we can call them 'artifacts' or 'goods' . . . are what eventually, over time, become part of the framework of the world for future generations."[6]

The church too generates artifacts and goods that become part of

3. James Davison Hunter, *To Change the World: The Irony, Tragedy, and Possibility of Christianity in the Late Modern World* (Oxford: Oxford University Press, 2010), 32, 45.
4. Lesslie Newbigin, *The Gospel in a Pluralist Society* (Grand Rapids: Eerdmans, 1989), 188.
5. Andy Crouch, *Culture Making: Recovering Our Creative Calling* (Downers Grove, IL: IVP, 2008), 24.
6. Crouch, *Culture Making*, 28.

the world for future generations. We form creeds and catechisms and doctrinal statements. We write hymns and songs. We baptize and marry and bury, creating rites and rituals in the process. We build buildings and preach sermons and send missionaries. In doing so, we create a culture—a shared universe, a world, a meaning-making matrix—that arises from us but that also exists outside of us.

Your church has a culture. So does mine. And the culture of our churches is saying something—about God, about us, about the gospel.

In an ideal world, the culture of every local church would reflect the glory of God, the lordship of Jesus, and the presence and power of the Holy Spirit. But a brief survey of the churches in the New Testament will remind you that we don't live in an ideal world. The church in Corinth was getting drunk at the Lord's Table and tolerating flagrant sexual sin among its members (1 Cor. 5:1–2; 11:20–21). The church in Ephesus had a penchant for embracing false doctrine and myths and speculation (1 Tim. 1:3–7). The church at Pergamum was awash in unbiblical teaching (Rev. 2:14–17).

These churches loved the gospel, just like we do. They were full of people who had been saved from sin by the death and resurrection of Jesus, just as we have. Yet they were marked by various kinds of worldliness and disorder. Why?

The simple answer, of course, is "sin." The fuller answer is that every person—and every local church—is enculturated.[7] Every Christian speaks a certain language, lives in a specific city, is a citizen of some nation, and has particular tastes in food and art and music. These aspects of culture—language, place, people, customs—reflect the more benign "image of God" realities of human life. But every culture also has its false gods. Just as the ancient Israelites tilted toward the worship of Baal or Asherah or Molech or Marduk depending on which nation was influencing them at the time, so

7. The ideas of enculturation and disenculturation are discussed by Richard Lovelace in *Dynamics of Spiritual Life: An Evangelical Theology of Renewal* (1970; repr., Downers Grove, IL: InterVarsity Press, 2020), 184–200.

modern Christians are prone to the lies and lusts most common in our cultures. We're citizens of God's kingdom, but we're also residents of this world, and we've been shaped by its influences.

This is why the first priority of the gospel is always repentance and faith. The first of Martin Luther's Ninety-Five Theses reads, "Our Lord and Master Jesus Christ, when he said, 'Repent,' willed that the whole life of believers should be repentance."[8] Churches can only reflect the beauty of the gospel if they practice repentance and faith, constantly turning from idols to serve the living and true God (1 Thess. 1:9). Each church must shed the worldly habits and values it has assimilated from the culture around it and be renewed according to the practices and patterns of the kingdom of God.

And that is why the work of cultural apologetics is crucial.

Changing How We See: Cultural Apologetics and Church Renewal

On July 8, 1879, George De Long (1844–81) and his crew of thirty-two explorers set sail from San Francisco in a quest to reach the North Pole. The scientific consensus at the time held that "the weather wasn't especially cold at the North Pole, at least not in summer. On the contrary, the dome of the world was covered in a shallow, warm, ice-free sea whose waters could be smoothly sailed, much as one might sail across the Caribbean or the Mediterranean."[9] The chief oceanographer of the US Navy agreed with this assessment, as did the world's most renowned cartographer. But as De Long's expedition tragically proved, the scientific consensus was entirely mistaken. De Long's men spent almost two years trapped in the Arctic. Their ship was rendered immobile and was eventually crushed by the ice

8. Martin Luther, *Works of Martin Luther*, trans. and ed. Adolph Spaeth et al. (Philadelphia: Holman, 1915), 1:29–38, https://www.projectwittenberg.org/pub/resources/text/wittenberg/luther/web/ninetyfive.html.

9. Hampton Sides, *In the Kingdom of Ice: The Grand and Terrible Polar Voyage of the USS Jeannette* (New York: Anchor, 2015), 43.

pack. Their last-ditch attempt to make it to Siberia in small lifeboats resulted in the deaths of twenty of the thirty-three sailors.

To us, it seems laughable to imagine balmy weather at the North Pole. But each moment in history has its own characteristic blindness. Our shared cultural assumptions don't even register as debatable. They're just "the way things are."

Spiritual blindness is one of the chief concerns of the Old Testament prophets. Elijah mocks the prophets of Baal for their elaborate rituals: "Cry aloud, for he is a god. Either he is musing, or he is relieving himself, or he is on a journey, or perhaps he is asleep and must be awakened" (1 Kings 18:27). Isaiah chides the idolaters of Babylon for the foolishness of their idolatry: "Over the half he eats meat; he roasts it and is satisfied. . . . And the rest of it he makes into a god, his idol, and falls down to it and worships it" (Isa. 44:16–17).

But the thing about blindness is that it's culturally reinforced. To the prophets of Baal and the pagans of Babylon, their idolatry didn't register as foolish precisely because it was culturally normal. From within the reigning plausibility structure of the time, it made sense. Only a God-given "word from outside" could help people see with new eyes.

Cultural apologetics plays a similar role in the life of the church. It unmasks cultural narratives, helping us see the foolish assumptions and false paradigms of our moment in history. We can then reject the idolatry of our culture, return to God in fresh repentance and faith, and rest again in the satisfying good news of God's grace in Jesus.

This work is vital to the renewal and reformation of the church. We who belong to Jesus Christ need our blindness exposed. We need our idols destroyed. We need disenculturation from the world around us. We need to be reminded that "the last word in human affairs is represented by a man hanging on a cross."

As this work of renewal happens in the church, it also begins to happen through the church.

Helping Others See: The Church as an Apologetic

My neighbor Evan (I've changed his name) is a successful, extroverted fortysomething: hip, engaging, friendly, and easy to talk to. He's always willing to lend a hand, an ear, or a tool. His kids are the most respectful and responsible middle-schoolers on the block. Evan and his wife know I'm a pastor; we've had them over for dinner; we do our best to initiate as much conversation and front-porch interaction as we can.

Yet Evan doesn't seem particularly curious about the deeper questions of life. He hasn't identified any God-shaped hole in his heart. It's not that he seems hardened or closed off to faith; he just doesn't appear to have any persistent spiritual hunger.

I sent Evan a text message to invite him to church this past Easter. He never responded.

I think a lot about Evan. I think about him when I preach: How would this message resonate with him? I think about him when I pray: How can I love him and witness to him more faithfully? And I think about him as I lead: How might I help him experience the church—and the gospel it proclaims—as interesting, compelling, and credible?

What I really want is for Evan to see the world differently. I want him to apprehend and be changed by the fact that "the last word in human affairs is represented by a man hanging on a cross."

It is God, of course, who must open Evan's eyes. But the Westminster Confession reminds us that "God, in His ordinary providence, makes use of means."[10] And one of those means is the church. I want my church—and your church—to give our neighbors a new set of "lenses" through which to see the world.

And we can. When churches take seriously our calling as countercultural communities, we start to do the work of cultural apologetics without even thinking about it! Because we love our

10. Westminster Confession of Faith 5.3, https://www.ligonier.org/learn/articles/westminster-confession-faith.

neighbors and want them to know Christ, we start thinking more intentionally about "how we do what we do." And without losing any of its depth and richness, what we do starts to reflect the transformative power of the gospel in ways that our neighbors often find compelling. Here are five ways that happens.

Preaching That Engages Doubt

"What therefore you worship as unknown, this I proclaim to you," Paul declared in Athens (Acts 17:23). He aimed his message at the gaps and idiosyncrasies in his hearers' worldview, graciously confronting their inconsistency. Effective preaching in our late-modern world follows the same pattern. The influence of postmodern epistemology and skepticism means we're all doubters now. A wise, evangelistically attuned approach to preaching seeks to reveal the flaws and gaps in modern ways of thinking, contrasting the weakness of cultural narratives with the strength and beauty of the gospel.

Editors often instruct journalists, "Show, don't tell." Compelling preaching does the same. It doesn't just tell people what the Bible says; it also shows the gospel to be more existentially satisfying, more intellectually compelling, and more situationally applicable than the cultural narratives on offer around us. This type of preaching takes its stand "between two worlds,"[11] confronting modern worldviews with Scripture while also putting the Bible in dialogue with modern concerns.

The church's preaching is an apologetic.

Hospitality That Welcomes the Outsider

Humans are distinctly aware of social cues. We quickly discern in-group and out-group dynamics, and we react accordingly.

11. *Between Two Worlds* was how British evangelical John Stott titled his famous book on Christian preaching, rooted in his observation that "a preaching ministry . . . [is] an activity of bridge-building between the revealed Word and the contemporary world." Stott, *Between Two Worlds: The Art of Preaching in the Twentieth Century* (Grand Rapids: Eerdmans, 1982), 178.

Churches that value theological orthodoxy can unintentionally create strong insider-outsider dichotomies: We place those who believe into one category and those who don't believe into another. But the gospel frees us to emphasize our common humanity without erasing or minimizing our differences. My neighbor Evan and I share much in common. We are husbands, fathers, and citizens. We work and play and eat and sleep. We pay taxes and cast votes and root for our favorite teams. We have hopes, dreams, fears, and uncertainties. We love, trust, and worship someone or something.

Churches that love the gospel highlight these shared human realities. They offer a genuine welcome to outsiders by emphasizing our common, shared humanity. This allows them to be bold and forthright in communicating the gospel, while also displaying humility and generosity toward fellow image-bearers.

The church's hospitality is an apologetic.

Worship That Shows the Arc of the Gospel

Years ago, a wise author posed a provocative question that changed the way I think about worship: "How is your worship service forming the expectations of the people who attend?" My answer was this: "It's teaching them to expect three fast songs, then two slow songs, then a sermon and a benediction." The church I served at the time was a standard evangelical megachurch with little connection to history and no real concern for catechesis. It relied on an emotionally powerful worship experience and a relevant and interesting sermon to do the work of Christian formation.

Thinking about my kids and my neighbors has changed my convictions about Christian worship. Our services now follow the "gospel arc" of historic Christian liturgy, which includes singing, corporate confession of sin, spoken creeds, the Lord's Prayer, and weekly Communion. The order of our worship service communicates something. It moves people along the story line of Scripture from creation to new creation. It works on an implicit, affective register, drawing people into a pattern of worship that helps them connect the dots of guilt, grace, and gratitude.

The church's worship is an apologetic.

Community That Rejoices in Repentance and Faith

A few years ago, I was invited to a local alumni club meeting for my alma mater. The gathering was held at a sports bar so we could watch our team play an important football game. It quickly became evident that the orienting center of this little community—the thing we gathered to rejoice in—was our football team.

Every community rejoices in something. And a gospel-oriented church rejoices in repentance and faith. We rejoice in confessing our sin, acknowledging our need, being honest about our weakness. We rejoice in the grace of Jesus Christ and the glory of God's promises in Scripture. And by rejoicing in these things, we become strangely countercultural.

A friend said to me recently, "Growing up, I never heard my dad apologize. He never admitted he was wrong about anything. When I first met some Christians, and they were confessing their sin to one another and asking for forgiveness, it radically affected me! I had never experienced that kind of humility."

The church's community is an apologetic.

Atmosphere of Resilient Hope

Suffering is the one experience guaranteed to every human being: "In this world you will have trouble" (John 16:33 NIV). And the gospel gives Christians a hearty resilience amid suffering. Paul and Silas, when imprisoned, sang hymns (Acts 16:25). Stephen, when martyred, forgave his attackers (7:60). And Peter, writing to the earliest Christians, urged them to "rejoice insofar as you share Christ's sufferings" (1 Pet. 4:13). Christians don't "grieve as others do who have no hope" (1 Thess. 4:13). Our grief is a hopeful grief.

Because a gospel-loving church is full of human beings, it will also be full of death and dementia and divorce and Down syndrome. These things come for us, just as they come for all the sons of Adam and daughters of Eve. But we face these things leaning forward in great hope, anticipating the resurrection of the dead and the life of the world to come. And that speaks volumes to a culture imprisoned by an "immanent frame."

The church's hope is an apologetic.

Embrace Our Calling

Throughout history, Christian theologians have reflected on the church's relationship to culture. Some writers emphasize the church's responsibility to confront culture. Others see the church as a leavening influence within culture. Still others emphasize the church's role as a counterculture.

When we realize that the church is a community of people who believe the gospel and live like it, we see that all three of these perspectives are true. The church exists to confront the world: "If the world hates you, know that it has hated me before it hated you" (John 15:18). The church exists as a transformative influence within society: "You are the salt of the earth. . . . You are the light of the world" (Matt. 5:13–14). And the church exists as a contrast community, an alternative kingdom to the kingdoms of this world: "Be blameless and innocent, children of God without blemish in the midst of a crooked and twisted generation, among whom you shine as lights in the world" (Phil. 2:15).

Since "the power which has the last word in human affairs is represented by a man hanging on a cross . . . the only hermeneutic of the gospel is a congregation of men and women who believe it and live like it."[12] The church doesn't just do apologetics; the church is an apologetic. May we embrace our calling and fulfill it to the glory of God.

12. Newbigin, *Gospel in a Pluralist Society*, 227.

12

Front Porches

Why We Still Need Them

JAMES P. EGLINTON

What is it like for post-Christendom Westerners to go to church for the first time? How do they make sense of what they see and hear there?

In a two-part series for Gospel in Life in 2023,[1] Tim Keller and I made the case that in our day, Western culture forms people—particularly religious "nones"—with a highly conflicted set of intuitions toward Christianity. Even in its current post-Christian phase, Western culture remains the product of a long and deep process of Christianization. Those raised within it, we argued, unwittingly imbibe Christian assumptions on a host of issues, which are held alongside a range of other (often

1. Tim Keller, "Lemonade on the Porch (Part 1): The Gospel in a Post-Christendom Society," Gospel in Life, Spring 2023. https://gospelinlife.com/article/gospel-in-a-post-christendom-society/; James Eglinton, "Lemonade on the Porch (Part 2)—Why and How to Build Porches: The Gospel in a Post-Christendom Society," Gospel in Life, Summer 2023, https://gospelinlife.com/article/lemonade-on-the-porch-part-2/.

explicitly) anti-Christian presuppositions. To people born into such a world, the first experience of church can be a jarring mix of the strikingly intuitive and the shockingly repugnant.

Recognizing that culture is a catechetical school for life's guiding intuitions (and that this is now true of Western culture in far-from-ideal ways), we made a plea to the church. First, it must recognize that mixed messages about Christianity are ingrained in the inner lives of those formed by present day Western culture. Second, in response, the church must create places where non-Christians can experience Christianity more holistically and thickly than now happens in mainstream culture. That experience must take place at the level of intuition and imagination, through the experience of relationships affected by the gospel (among Christians, and between Christians and their non-Christian neighbors) and have scope to progress from the *implicit experience* of Christianity to *explicit discussion* of how and why it shapes life in particular ways.

Our argument was that such microcultures must exist outside the gathered worship of the church. Aptly, Keller described them as "porches" midway between the church and the street. This chapter supplements those articles by setting out why churches need porches. It does so primarily by highlighting the earlier contribution of Abraham Kuyper (whose writings prompted us toward the view that porches will play an increasingly important role in making the first experience of church different for post-Christendom Westerners). It will conclude with a series of practical suggestions for porch builders.

Our cultural moment may feel new to some Christians in the West. But as we'll see with Kuyper more than one hundred years ago, we're not alone in considering our response to the post-Christendom era.

Westerners at Church

The West, of course, is a large and diverse place. It almost goes without saying that many people across Western Europe, North America, and the Antipodes inhabit (often globe-spanning) religious communities and subcultures. Alongside these, however, a vast number of Westerners also identify as religious "nones." Such people are found from Auckland to Edinburgh, Atlanta to Vancouver. Many use that label to express personal rejection of a prior religious affiliation. Many others use it to describe a life that has never had anything to do with religions of the label-wearing, organized sort. In Scotland, where I live, it is easy to find adult religious "nones" who have never read a Bible or been to a church, school children who don't know whose birth is celebrated at Christmas, and so on.

That lack of experience doesn't mean that by default, Westernized religious "nones" live out a strictly atheistic materialism. In universal theological terms, they are made in the image of God and constantly receive (and suppress) his general revelation in their inner lives (Rom. 1:18–19). For that reason, we shouldn't be surprised to find that being a religious "none" often goes hand in hand with all kinds of self-directed religiosity. Alongside this, as was noted at the outset, a person can have no direct knowledge or experience of Christianity while also being profoundly, unwittingly affected by it.

The Dutch missiologist J. H. Bavinck described twentieth-century Western Europe as lit by the nameless afterglow of Christianity in the lives of its many purportedly irreligious (and even anti-Christian) inhabitants. "Worldviews," he wrote, "last for longer than one generation. One generation can celebrate worldviews that provide no foundation for its own life and without that generation's exterior taking on noticeable damage. This is so because for all of us, our hearts are unconsciously so Christian."[2] This particular insight is important as we ask a question: In culture-specific terms, what kinds of experiences do irreligious (which is to say, culturally post-Christendom) Westerners have when observing a church service for the first time? And in light

2. J. H. Bavinck, *Personality and Worldview*, ed. and trans. James Eglinton (Wheaton, IL: Crossway, 2023).

of that experience, *how can Christians better help their unchurched neighbors prepare for that experience in advance*? And on that basis, how do churches in that context reach such people?

Generational Shift

One of the first modern European theologians to pose this question was Abraham Kuyper, the early twentieth-century Dutch neo-Calvinist.[3] Dutch society had undergone its own dechurching across the nineteenth century, the era in which Kuyper came of age. As a fruit of that century, a new demographic appeared: those who professed no religion at all. Writing in 1910, Kuyper drew on census results from the previous year in which some 80,000 people declared themselves to be religious "nones."[4] In a country of 5.5 million, that demographic was small. However, Kuyper expected their number to grow, particularly given their emergence against a backdrop of generally declining rates of church attendance.

In Kuyper's view, the emergence of post-Christendom religious "nones" was historically novel and needed focused attention. "We will make it impossible to work effectively on them," he argued, "if we do not make a more serious attempt to comprehend and understand their lack of religion. . . . The question is . . . whether the influences tempering or fostering this [lack of religion] now work in an entirely different manner compared to before."[5] In exploring this question, Kuyper provided a grand sweep of Western history. In that

3. For an introduction to Kuyper, see James Bratt, *Abraham Kuyper: Modern Calvinist, Christian Democrat* (Grand Rapids: Eerdmans, 2013); Richard Mouw, *Abraham Kuyper: A Short and Personal Introduction* (Grand Rapids: Eerdmans, 2011); and Robert Joustra and Jessica Joustra, eds., *Calvinism for a Secular Age: A Twenty-First Century Reading of Kuyper's Stone Lectures* (Downers Grove, IL: IVP Academic, 2022).
4. Abraham Kuyper, *Pro Rege 1: Living Under Christ the King*, trans. Albert Gootjes (Bellingham, WA: Lexham, 2016), 13.
5. Kuyper, *Pro Rege 1*, 44. In probing this, Kuyper touched on an idea similar to Taylor's "conditions of belief." See Charles Taylor, *A Secular Age* (Boston, MA: Belknap, 2007), 539–617.

history, for many centuries, Europeans living under the conditions of Christendom experienced life in the world that generally corresponded to the experience of churchgoing (as was still the case for Muslims in Islamic societies, Kuyper wrote, when transferring from everyday life to the experience of Friday prayers).[6] Life in the world assumed a sacred order rooted in Christian theology. Even if it was mostly unpronounced, that order grounded the practice of everyday life in Christian intuitions about God and self, good and evil, forgiveness and grace, embodiment, hope, the afterlife, and so on. Although most medieval Europeans only attended church infrequently, when they did so, Christian worship both chimed with that sacred order and also made more sense of ordinary life. Direct engagement with Christianity was an affirmation of that person's general formation in the surrounding culture. It was not a jarring experience in that sense. Rather, the opposite was true: It had resonant affective power because it was met with relatively little culturally ingrained resistance.

In 1910, Kuyper saw that things had changed dramatically—particularly for the teenagers of his day. Europe-wide cultural Christendom, that warm bath of implicit Christianity, was gone. With that shift, he thought, Dutch culture could no longer be assumed to be any kind of reliable formative environment for those who would then experience the church.

In describing that change, however, Kuyper didn't entertain a simplistic sense of Western culture as having moved from a pro-Christian to an anti-Christian phase. Human beings, and the deep entanglement of Christianity through Western culture, were much too complicated for that. Rather, he saw European culture as having become simultaneously proreligious and antireligious, cherishing some aspects of Christianity while despising others. The apex of that confusion, he believed, was *Christological*: Secularized Europeans could appreciate a sense in which Jesus is Savior but not that Christ is King.

6. Kuyper, *Pro Rege 1*, 3–12.

A range of modern thinkers supposed that as Savior, Christ benefited humanity in one way or another—as an elevated moral teacher, an example of love or sacrifice, and so on.[7] The notion that Jesus is also King of kings, however, was more problematic. Self-confident, self-assertive modern Europeans found less to salvage from that particular claim. That mentality produced people who, however inchoately, were willing to receive from Jesus but not to render anything to him in return. To such people, a first experience with the church will be jarring indeed. It will be intuitive in the sense that Jesus offers them himself and counterintuitive in all he demands of them.

Kuyper's description of the bygone days of Christendom were part of a general historical picture in which *culture* had always existed in relationship to *cultus* (i.e., worship). To be sure, a culture and its object of worship are somewhat different things. Culture is loose, inarticulate, and carries people passively, whereas the worship at its center is articulate, focused, and more demanding of heart and mind.[8] The church's strange predicament in the modern West, however, was that it continued to exist as a worshiping community but was now surrounded by a culture that gave people such conflicted intuitions toward it. In that sense, the modern West (as a product of centuries of Christianization) was exceptional in comparison to the cultures shaped by and pointing toward Islam, Buddhism, and Confucianism. For followers of those religions, he supposed, life in those cultures was much less conflicted and far more holistic than in the modern West, where the lives of many were culture without cultus.

Formation in that kind of culture makes for a confusing first meeting with Christianity. Here, we could update Kuyper with the example of a modern-day religious "none" who encounters

7. For an exploration of Kuyper's interactions with a range of modern philosophers and theologians on this, see James Eglinton, "Kuyper on Religion," in Joustra and Joustra, *Calvinism for a Secular Age*, 32–51.

8. Kuyper, *Pro Rege 1*, 41.

Christianity for the first time and finds the combination of God's grace and righteousness deeply perplexing. As a product of a culture that normalizes unconditional self-acceptance, the Westerner is not immediately repelled by the idea that God might also accept a person unconditionally. Alongside this, though, the idea that God also stands in judgment over him, and even demands his repentance and obedience, might be shockingly counterintuitive. Someone in that position might well struggle to intuit whether Christianity is good or bad news. What, then, can Christians do to help prepare such people for a first encounter with the faith?

Forecourts and Holy Places

To describe this proposal, Kuyper drew on a biblical image: The Old Testament temple had both a holy place and a forecourt. That forecourt was, in effect, a formative cultural space lacking the intensity, intentionality, and sharpness of mind and heart that came with entering the holy place. But it was nonetheless marked by that holy place and prepared people for it. In that sense, cultural Christendom formerly served as a distinctive kind of forecourt to the holy place of the church. In that age's cultural forecourt, people felt less mastery over nature, more threatened by disease and precarity, and less drunk on individual wealth. This lack was conducive to the experience of calling upon God as almighty Father. In the modern age, the character of the surrounding cultural forecourt changed dramatically on each of those points. The modern person reimagined himself as the master of his world, unraveling its mysteries and solving its ills through science. He fulfilled his every whim through the power of money (which he had changed from a finite, physical commodity to an almost infinite, invisible source of power). Those changes made it harder for Westernized people in general to engage with church.

For that reason, Kuyper noted that modern-day Christians and religious "nones" swim in the same murky cultural water.[9] The effect on committed Christians is considerable: In complex ways, their experience of holy place and forecourt, of culture and cultus, is also jarring. In the holy place, we're confronted by the living God; in the forecourt, God is widely assumed to be an optional extra. Moving between those places takes a toll.[10]

This chapter focuses, though, on those who have only ever milled around in the forecourt—secularized Western people who might attend church for the first time in adulthood and who have been primed by modern Western culture to have a distinctively conflicted response to that experience. Although Kuyper had much to say on this experience, it was as a cultural analyst rather than as a missiologist. Nonetheless, his writings lay down a missiological challenge: What should the church do when the culture around it no longer serves as a reliable forecourt, when the basics of intuition and imagination it forms in people will leave them struggling to know what to make of the gospel? This was the task Keller and I took up.

Cultural Apologetics on the Porch

As part of the biblical task of persuasive gospel presentation (Acts 18:4), cultural apologetics aims to help people see that their responses to that message are always culturally contingent and local, rather than equally compelling to all people everywhere.[11] In this sense, Paul described the different starting points of Jews who "demand signs" and Greeks who "seek wisdom" and the ways those starting

9. Kuyper, *Pro Rege 1*, 43.
10. On this point, Kuyper's argument is not far from Charles Taylor's more recent picture of secularized people—believers and unbelievers—as living differently fragmented, "cross pressured" lives in which both are subject to secularization, albeit in distinct ways. See Taylor, *A Secular Age*, 594–617.
11. See also Timothy Keller, *Center Church: Doing Balanced, Gospel-Centered Ministry in Your City* (Grand Rapids: Zondervan, 2012), 89–134.

points lead to different ways of rejecting the gospel: To Jews it is a "stumbling block," whereas to Greeks it is "folly" (1 Cor. 1:22–23).

In that approach, the apologist highlights that whatever a particular non-Christian's reasons for rejecting the gospel, that non-Christian would find his own objections unpersuasive if he were born in a different culture or time. (Kuyper used this argument, telling irreligious teens in 1910 that their beliefs would have been radically different had they been born in the Middle Ages.) Cultural apologetics explains to non-Christian Westerners why they respond to the gospel as they do—simultaneously finding parts of its content intuitive and familiar, while other aspects strike them as untenable and offensive. This task (resourced by the works of Glen Scrivener, Tom Holland, and Larry Siedentop)[12] plays its own role in preparing non-Christians for a first experience of church and does so by helping them approach Christianity with a clearer sense of who they are as non-Christians. In a sense, such writing serves as a kind of literary forecourt. Important as it is, though, literature of that sort isn't the sum total of the forecourt space.

A key part of Kuyper's argument for the evangelistic benefit of Christendom was that it allowed nominal cultural Christians to experience something of the fruits of the faith in an embodied, communal form before engaging with church directly. The culture let them passively belong, and the church asked them to actively believe. As noted at the outset, Keller adapted that concept in a strikingly American way: The church needs *porches*, "half-way places between the insides of the homes and the streets."[13] On the porch, before passersby cross the front door, they can experience something of the life of the home within. And from the porch, the life of the household becomes attentive to the needs of the street and could even influence

12. On this, see Glen Scrivener, *The Air We Breathe: How We All Came to Believe in Freedom, Kindness, and Equality* (Epson, UK: Good Book, 2022); Tom Holland, *Dominion: The Making of the Western Mind* (New York: Basic, 2019); Larry Siedentop, *Inventing the Individual: The Origins of Western Liberalism* (Boston: Harvard University Press, 2014).
13. Keller, "Lemonade on the Porch (Part 1)."

it for good. Keller's vision of porches was primarily *relational*. Porches are places in which non-Christians can see the gospel affecting how Christians relate to one another (and to them), where they can ask questions (as a way of beginning to understand Christianity on its own terms, as well as coming to see the cultural narratives that shape their own lives), and where Christianity is presented to them with contextual specificity.[14]

That insistence is important in clarifying what a porch isn't. It isn't a catchall term for every form of public outreach. While some contexts might allow churches to hold open-air services in public places, for example, the wholesale relocation of a worship service like that doesn't necessarily turn it into a porch.[15] (A religious "none" attending an open-air service for the first time will have the same conflicted response, regardless of the venue.) Similarly, although a church stall in a public place handing out leaflets with information on its Sunday services is a valuable endeavor (and implicitly communicates important things about Christianity), it isn't necessarily a porch. If a passerby does not engage with the Christians at the stall, but takes a leaflet and happens to visit a service, the stall will not have prepared her to intuit Christianity in the way a porch would. By definition, a porch invites people to experience (and then discuss) a community of relationships infused by the gospel before they attend church—an unusual experience of community that the church then sets in context.

That can happen, Keller suggested, in Christian schools that take on non-Christian students, in Christian ministries that meet the needs of the poor, and in small-group book clubs that expect non-Christians to participate. To give a personal example of a porch

14. Eglinton, "Lemonade on the Porch (Part 2)."
15. It is possible, of course, to conduct public worship in ways that incorporate "porches" directly in the liturgy. Keller recognised, for example, that preaching can contain "porch" elements in so far as it both communicates the gospel *and* explains to hearers that their initial response to it is an expression of culturally contingent, localized forms of idolatry. Eglinton, "Lemonade on the Porch (Part 2)."

in action, last year I attended a public lecture by a Christian writer held in an Edinburgh hotel. The Christian organization responsible invited a wide range of people, Christians and non-Christians, and encouraged free and charitable questions for the speaker. In the Q&A, some Christians in the audience disagreed with (and challenged) the speaker, who also welcomed questions from non-Christians. After the event, I stood in conversation with an atheist friend and a group of Christians who were discussing their own differing views on the lecture. My atheist friend was taken aback by the ease with which Christians could handle disagreement and somehow stay friends: "Intellectually, my people are left-wing secular progressives," she said, "but there, it's all about 'purity of thought,' and nobody dares to say what they really think because if you get it wrong, you're out. Socially, I feel like my people are Christians, because here we can actually talk like this." It was a conversation on a porch and a brief experience of community. I hope that if my friend were to step beyond the porch, into the house itself, she would not be surprised to find Christians worshiping a God who is supremely hospitable and in no way brittle.

There are many ways to build such porches, with abundant scope for complexity and scale. A high-profile event like a public lecture in a hotel takes resources and planning and assumes a prior network of friendships between Christians and their neighbors. Not all porches need that level of organization. Keller's own final reminder was that the original New Testament porch "was simply a highly hospitable Christian home, a place to which non-believing neighbors and colleagues are constantly invited and where Christian faith is unselfconsciously modeled and discussed."[16] In that sense, as Gray Sutanto's chapter in this book reminds us, the work of cultural apologetics is certainly not limited to professional apologists, pastors, and theologians.

It begins, in all simplicity, in the home.

---

16. Keller, "Lemonade on the Porch (Part 1)."

13

Everyday Life

The Cultural Texts We Live By

SAM CHAN

The winters in Chicago are cold and bleak. I know because my wife and I lived there for five years. During these winters there is much to be gloomy about. The sidewalks are icy, the skies are grey, and the roads are dangerous. But then the most amazing thing happens in spring: Thousands and thousands of tulips bloom. The main street of Chicago, Michigan Avenue, becomes a ribbon of spectacular colors—pinks, yellows, reds—and soon our gloom is replaced by joy.

This happens because Chicago has a tradition where it plants tulip bulbs each year just before winter arrives. That way, we can survive the winter, knowing that the tulip bulbs are there, buried beneath the snow, waiting for their time to blossom. And blossom they will!

In the same way, we can say there are "seeds of the gospel" buried in every culture's story lines. Or as C. S. Lewis puts it, God has placed "good dreams" in the stories cultures tell.[1] This means that, in every culture, no matter how godless, there are seeds of the gospel—buried, lurking, and waiting for their time to blossom. It also means that, for believers, there are opportunities everywhere to identify these "seeds of the gospel." In every conversation, in every situation, in every location, no matter how godless, there will be "seeds of the gospel" for us to nurture and grow into gospel conversations with our nonbelieving friends.

So how can we do this? Here we can learn from the example of Paul in Athens, as recorded in Acts 17.

"Wow! You Have a Lot of Idols"

In verse 16, Paul enters Athens, which is brimming with idols. It's difficult to imagine a more God-less cultural story line than this, but somehow Paul finds a way to uncover the seeds of the gospel buried in it. He then nurtures and grows these seeds into a fully blossomed gospel conversation.

Yes, but how?

First, Paul *observes* that Athens is full of idols. We can imagine him saying to a local Athenian, "Wow! You have a lot of idols." In doing so, Paul describes the Athenian's cultural text—in this case, the idols—on its own terms, idioms, and metaphors.[2] The Athenian might reply, "Yep. We sure do. We have a lot of idols." The local person nods and agrees with Paul's correct observation.

1. C. S. Lewis, *Mere Christianity* (New York: Touchstone, 1980), 54.
2. Cultures create "texts" to express their story lines. Those texts don't have to be written. They can be anything that expresses the culture's worldview—from poems, fashion, art, songs, gardens, buildings, sports, hairstyles, movies, and so on. For more on "cultural texts," see Kevin J. Vanhoozer, "What Is Everyday Theology? How and Why Christians Should Read Culture," in *Everyday Theology: How to Read Cultural Texts and Interpret Trends*, ed. Kevin J. Vanhoozer, Charles A. Anderson, and Michael J. Sleasman (Grand Rapids: Baker, 2007), 26.

Second, Paul *understands* the existential cry[3] behind the Athenian's cultural text, the idols. Paul says, "I see that in every way you are very religious" (v. 22 NIV). In doing so, Paul interprets the meaning behind the idols: The Athenians are looking to connect with the transcendent. They cry out to worship and appease the gods behind the universe.

Third, Paul *empathizes* with this cultural story line, "I even found an altar with this inscription: TO AN UNKNOWN GOD" (v. 23 NIV). The Athenians are so desperate to worship and appease the gods that they even have an altar set aside for an unknown god, just in case they've left out any. Paul doesn't ridicule this. Instead, he empathizes with their desperation. We can imagine Paul saying, "Who of us wouldn't want this to be true? Who wouldn't want to cover all our bases? We want to make sure we worship and appease each and every god."

Fourth, Paul *deconstructs* their cultural story line. He does this by demonstrating a *deficiency* in their story line—there's something missing. For example, the Athenians don't know the name of this God. How can they worship a God whose name they don't know? Paul also does this by demonstrating the *dissonance* in their story line—there's something clashing. That is, the Athenians believe in two things that can't be true at the same time. For example, the Athenians claim this God is unknown, yet their own authors say he is nearby: "For in him we live and move and have our being," and "We are his offspring" (v. 28 NIV). So which is it? Is he unknown or knowable? Or, as another example, the Athenians believe this unknown God made the universe, but at the same time they try to contain him in a temple (v. 24).

Fifth, Paul *fulfills* their cultural story line with the gospel. Paul

3. For me, an existential cry is a God-given, legitimate cry for transcendence and connection with God, as hinted in Ecclesiastes 3:11: "[God] has put eternity into man' s heart." Daniel Strange calls this the "magnetic sticking point" in *Making Faith Magnetic: Five Hidden Themes Our Culture Can't Stop Talking About . . . and How to Connect Them to Christ* (Epsom: Good Book, 2021).

offers to tell them the name of the God whose name they don't know (v. 23). He tells them they can know their unknown God and will show them how to worship the God who is bigger than their temple.

So Paul does the following:

1. Observes a cultural text: "Wow. You have a lot of idols."
2. Understands their existential cry: "I see that you are very religious. You even have an altar to an unknown God."
3. Empathizes with their cultural story line: "Who of us wouldn't want this to be true?"
4. Deconstructs their cultural story line: "But you don't know the name of this God."
5. Fulfills their cultural story line: "Let me tell you the name of this God."

Let's see what this could look like for us in everyday life.

Weekend Children's Sports

Let's begin with the cultural phenomenon of children's sports. All over the world, thousands of kids play sports. And every weekend, parents clog the streets to drive them there, volunteer to be on coaching or canteen duties, and stand shoulder-to-shoulder on sidelines to cheer on their kids. In the same way that Athens was brimming with idols, our culture is brimming with children's sports on the weekend.

Let's say we're one of those parents on the sideline. What might a gospel conversation sound like here?

First, we can say to another parent standing next to us, "Wow. There sure is a lot of children's sports this weekend." In doing so, we observe that children's sports is a cultural text. Of course, our conversation wouldn't be as wooden as I've just described. For example, I can say, "I've got three kids, and I've got three games to get to today. How about you?" After a while, I can say, "We sure have a lot of children's sports in our life." We can easily imagine the other parent nodding and responding, "Yep. We sure do."

Second, we understand the existential cry that causes us to sign up our kids for children's sports. We can say, "I guess it's better than our kids staying at home and playing on their screens. There's something good about being outdoors." In doing so, we understand that, deep down, we want our children to do well. We believe sports is good for our children. It might even help them "get ahead" in life.

Third, we empathize with this story line. We can say, "Sports makes us so busy with all the running around, but I can see how it's good for my children. They get fit. And they make friends." It's a great story line that promises our children not just fitness and health, but also validation, success, and advancement. Who among us doesn't want this to be true?

Fourth, we deconstruct the story line. We can say, "But it's a shame so much of sports is about winning. After all, it's not like most of our kids are going on to a professional career in this sport. We keep telling our kids that it's not about the winning, but it's still so easy to obsess over winning every single game." Here we demonstrate the dissonance that is integral to children's sports. We know it's not about winning, and we tell our kids this. Yet many parents still scream at their kids to do better and argue loudly with referees over questionable calls. So why is it so much about the winning?

Fifth, we fulfill the cultural story line with Jesus. We can say, "I guess sports is a metaphor for the universe. In the big bad real world, we do have to be the biggest, fastest, and strongest. Otherwise we get eaten alive. In a godless universe, it's only about winning, but deep down, we know that's not true. After all, this is what we tell our children. But this can only be true if the God of the Bible is true. Because it's only the God of the Bible who sends his Son Jesus to show that life isn't about 'survival of the fittest.' Jesus became the smallest, weakest, and meekest for our sake. Life doesn't belong to the strongest. It belongs to those who serve and worship. If so, sports is a way of serving the community and worshiping the God who provides good things—like sports!—for us to enjoy."

Can you see how we've moved from sports to the gospel in the same way Paul moved from idols to Jesus? As I mentioned, in real life, the conversation will not be so wooden and formulaic. It will be messy and organic. The above imaginary conversation can take place over ten minutes or ten weeks, but no matter the timeline, these are the steps we can take to guide a conversation eventually to Jesus.

Fitness Trackers

Let's now enter the world of fitness trackers. Many of us carry fitness trackers to count how many steps we take per day. Whether we wear stand-alone devices on our wrists, use our smart watches to count our steps, or use our phones to do so, in the matter of only a few years, we've become obsessed with counting our steps. Usually, "ten thousand steps" is the objective marker of being active enough for one day. In the same way that Athens was overrun by idols, we're now overrun with the cultural phenomenon of ten thousand steps.

Let's say we glance at our friend who's wearing a fitness tracker. What can a gospel conversation sound like here?

First, we can say to our friend, "Wow. There sure are a lot of fitness trackers these days." Again, a real conversation wouldn't be so formulaic. Instead, I could say, "I see you have a fitness tracker. Tell me more."

Second, we understand the existential cry that makes us count our steps. We can say, "I use my watch to count my steps. I want to make sure I move enough for the day. How about you?" In doing so, we understand that we want to stay active. We have an existential cry for health, fitness, beauty, perfection, and achievement.

Third, we empathize with this story line. We can say, "It's good to have a goal—ten thousand steps!—to know if I've done enough for the day." It's an empowering message that says we can control our fitness destiny. The only thing holding us back is our lack of steps, but if we reach our goal of ten thousand, then we can be fitter, slimmer, and healthier. Who of us doesn't want this to be true?

Fourth, we deconstruct the story line. We can say, "But it does make you wonder why it has to be ten thousand steps. Why is it ten thousand steps and not 9,500 steps? Or 200 steps?" Ten thousand steps is an arbitrary, made-up number deliberately designed to make us feel like we're never doing enough. Our cultural story line always creates benchmarks of achievements, self-improvement, and perfection. Every day we need eight hours of sleep, two servings of vegetables . . . and ten thousand steps. The problem is, we regularly fall short. These benchmarks disempower and ultimately discourage us. We can never be good enough for our society's standard of perfection.

Fifth, we fulfill the cultural story line with Jesus. We can say, "This is where my Christian faith gives me relief from the daily reminders that I haven't done enough. God sent us his Son Jesus to be our new benchmark of perfection. Even better, Jesus both achieves the perfect life for us and empowers us to be perfect by placing his Spirit in us. That's why Jesus cries out, 'It's done!' when he dies for us on the cross. In Jesus, we will always have done enough. In Jesus, God sees us as perfect."

Watching a Movie

We often watch movies with our friends. So how can we move from movies to the gospel in the same way that Paul moves from idols to Jesus? Let's choose the movie *Top Gun: Maverick* (2022) as an example. If you haven't seen this sequel to the 1986 movie *Top Gun*, the hero, Maverick, is played by Tom Cruise, and it's about flying fighter jets for the US Navy.

I choose this movie because it has a story line that's common to most big-budget action movies and because it's the highest-grossing film in Tom Cruise's career—$1.5 billion worldwide. This means many of us have seen this movie, and there must've been something attractive about this story line for so many of us to go watch it.

After watching *Top Gun: Maverick* with our friend, how can our conversation go?

First, we can say to our friend, "Wow. What a movie!" Perhaps we can mention that the movie did well worldwide. Millions of people all over the world happily watched this movie. And we can ask our friend what they enjoyed about the movie.

Second, we understand the existential cry behind the movie's cultural story line. We can say, "Did you notice it was all about the need for a mission? Maverick is good at flying planes, but there's no point unless he can find a mission." When Maverick is grounded, he's miserable. We need to answer the question, "Why am I here?"

Third, we empathize with this cultural story line by saying, "Who of us doesn't feel the same?" For example, we also feel the same pointlessness of work, study, and play, unless we can answer the question, "Why am I here?" Without a mission, we're also miserable.

Fourth, we deconstruct the cultural story line. We can say, "But did you notice that the movie can't stand alone?" That's because, before we see the movie, our friends who recommend it tell us we must first see the original *Top Gun* (1986) for the sequel to make sense. Without the *bigger* story, it's only fast planes and good-looking actors. No story can stand alone. Every story needs to be part of a bigger story. But if this is true, where's our bigger story? Without a bigger story, our life is also only a series of events that happen, but with no rhyme or reason.

Fifth, we fulfill the cultural story line with the gospel. If Maverick needs a mission, we do too. If *Top Gun: Maverick* needs a bigger story, then we do too. But if this is only a godless universe of matter and chance, then there's no such thing as a mission or story. We can say, "What we need is a God who sends us his Son Jesus to be our Story. And that's exactly what we have in the pages of the Bible: God's story for us." We can show them John 1:14, which announces that "the Word became Flesh." That is, Jesus is God's Story for us, coming to us, so we can now be part of God's bigger story. In Jesus, we will find our mission and purpose.

Catching a Plane

Air travel has become routine for many of us. Thousands catch planes for work or family vacations and clog the airports during the major holidays. In the same way Athens was overloaded with idols, our culture is overloaded with planes. But here's the thing: Very few of us enjoy catching planes. For most of us, it's a drag.

Let's say we're catching a plane with friends. How can this conversation go?

First, we can say to our friend, "Wow. Catching planes is a drag." We're observing the cultural phenomenon of how air travel is now a mundane, unpleasant activity. It's a painful ritual of getting to the airport, going through security, sitting in a cramped seat next to a stranger, and waiting for baggage. I rarely see anyone smiling at an airport, especially while they wait for their baggage.

Second, we understand the existential cry for a better way to travel. We long for comfort, consistency, and convenience, yet air travel fails to deliver. It gives us the opposite: planes that are uncomfortable, unreliable, and inconvenient.

Third, we empathize with this cultural story line that cries out for a better way. We can say, "One day, they'll invent a better way to travel. Our grandchildren will look back at us and feel sorry for us." It's a great story line that promises inventions, innovation, and progress. Who of us doesn't want a better way to travel?

Fourth, we can deconstruct the story line by saying, "But wait! What are we saying? For thousands of years humankind was trying to fly. But now we can! We can do what ancient civilizations could only dream of doing. Why do we now find it a drag?" This shows that the human condition always longs for more. Even if, one day, we could travel by laser beam, fly to Mars, or cure the common cold, we would still be underwhelmed by it.

Fifth, we fulfill the cultural story line with Jesus. We can say, "This shows that our greatest need isn't for more comfort, toys, or inventions. We will still long for more. Our greatest need is eternal life." We can tell our friend the story of Jesus meeting a man who had everything (Mark 10:17–31). But he lacked one thing: Jesus! Jesus is better than whatever we think will make us happy, and only he can give us the "something more" our heart desires. Jesus gives us eternal life.

Doing the Laundry

There can be nothing more mundane or godless than doing the laundry! Yet this is something we find ourselves doing regularly. It's also something we may do with a friend if we live in shared accommodation. Or it's something we talk about with friends when we complain about the busyness of life. So how can we move from the laundry to the gospel?

First, we can say to our friend, "Wow. We sure do a lot of laundry." We're observing the cultural phenomenon of how doing the laundry is part of our everyday, mundane existence. We regularly load washing machines, unload them, hang clothes to dry, load dryers, unload them, take down clothes from the line, fold clothes, iron them, and put folded clothes away in the drawer. Only to do it all over again. And again. And again. We can easily imagine our friend nodding vigorously and replying, "Yep. We sure do."

Second, we understand the existential cry that causes us to wash, dry, fold, and iron our clothes every day. We can say, "Laundry is such a boring part of our daily life, but I can see why we have to do it." In doing so, we show that deep down we long for purposeful activity.

Third, we empathize with the cultural story line. We can say, "It's worth it for the clean clothes to wear." This story line promises that, no matter how painful or mundane our activity, if there's purpose—in this case, clean clothes—then it will be worth doing. Without purpose, we only have an answer to the question "What am I doing?" but we lack an answer to the question "Why am I doing it?"

Fourth, we deconstruct the story line. We can say, "But have you ever wondered what is the purpose of our life? We have an answer to the question 'What am I?' I'm a human being. But we don't have an answer to the question 'Why am I here?' Without purpose, our life is more meaningless than our laundry. At least we know why we do the laundry. But we don't know why we exist."

Fifth, we fulfill the cultural story line with Jesus. We can say, "Without God there really can be no purpose outside of ourselves. But with the God of the Bible, we find our purpose in Jesus. Jesus is the 'Why?' to my existence." In the same way it's worth doing the laundry, our life will also be worth living because of Jesus.

We Can Do This

I remember the first time I tried to poach an egg. It was somewhat messy. But I've done it a few more times, and now I've gotten the hang of it. Cultural apologetics in everyday life is like poaching an egg.

In the same way Paul wanders into Athens and says, "I see that you're very religious," we can have a coffee with a friend and say, "I see that you have a fitness tracker on your wrist," and take it from there. The first few times we do this, it might feel messy, but eventually we will get the hang of it.

But it's even better than poaching an egg. As Paul says in 2 Corinthians 2:14, we're spreading "the aroma" of Christ (NIV). In fact, we ourselves in everyday life will exude this aroma. Sooner or later, we will become Christ's cultural text to our friends, and in us, they'll see the better story of Jesus.

Conclusion

The Narrow Road to Eternal Life

COLLIN HANSEN

Vladimir Putin didn't catch many by surprise when his Russian army invaded Ukraine in 2022. He had been amassing tanks and infantry on the border for months, after all. Many were surprised, however, by the rationale he gave for the invasion.

He promised to de-Nazify Russia's southwestern neighbor.

Guffaws could be heard across the West. Invading—unprovoked—a neighboring European country led by a Jewish president seemed like just about the most Nazi thing you could do. But in Russian memory, repelling Nazi aggression is the great national story, the narrative that unites disparate peoples across vast lands.

Culture is created by narrative. The stories we tell become the values we live by.

"We owe our happiness to the salvation of the past," Byung-Chul Han writes in *The Crisis of Narration*. "This salvation requires a narrative tension in which the present integrates the past, thereby making the past a continuing influence, even resurrecting the past."[1]

In other words, if Russians are de-Nazifying Ukraine, then their

1. Byung-Chul Han, *The Crisis of Narration* (Hoboken, NJ: Polity, 2024), 16–17.

cause is just, and they will prevail no matter how long it takes, no matter how many people die. The invasion has been sanctified by the blood of patriots past.

This book has explored how secular, immanent narratives have replaced the Christian, transcendent story in the Western imagination. And we have considered various ways Christians might advocate for our faith today, in humility before the past, with hope toward the future. As we conclude, let us consider the most widespread historical narrative of our day and the implications for cultural apologetics. For the West has reached a crossroads. And only one road can lead us to safety from the devils lurking in our past, seeking to devour our present.

One Cross to Another

When Putin reaches back more than eighty years for justification, he's acknowledging the weakness of his political agenda today.

"Because we lack sufficiently strong communal narratives, our late-modern societies are unstable," Han writes. "Without a shared narrative, the *political*, which makes *shared action* possible, cannot properly form."[2]

In the aftermath of communism, Putin restored many privileges of the Russian Orthodox Church, whose spiritual authority he enlisted in his war against Ukraine. But no one seriously thinks Moscow's priests could challenge Putin, like the Old Testament prophet Nathan challenged King David. The state today is secular, and the church serves at the state's privilege.

This story of secularism, or how the West moved past historic Christian concepts of God, could be told at many different layers. We might reach back all the way to the Axial Age to find wrestling between immanence and transcendence in the sixth century before

2. Han, *Crisis of Narration*, 64.

the coming of Christ.[3] We could look at the sixteenth century after Christ when the stand of a solitary German monk shattered Rome's pretensions to rule Christendom.[4] We could examine political revolutions that began in the United States and later tore down the church in France and Russia, two historic pillars of Christendom. Or we could look at the precipitous drop in religiosity, especially in the United States, just since the widespread adoption of the internet since the turn of the twenty-first century.[5]

But perhaps the most common story of secularism we tell and retell ourselves is the Second World War. Durham University historian Alec Ryrie examines resonant cultural symbols. Before the Soviet Union and Nazi Germany invaded Poland in 1939, the symbol most resonant across the West was the cross of Christ. Ever since, a different cross—one known by Hindus and Buddhists for centuries before Adolf Hitler adopted it for his Nazi Party—evokes more powerful responses.

For Ryrie, this change narrates the failure of Christendom to prevent the Second World War and especially the Holocaust. Christianity and its petty rules of moral decorum couldn't shut down the gas chambers at Treblinka. Few today bother to even wonder what Jesus would do. But they try not to be as bad as Hitler.[6] And making Hitler out to be a singularly evil figure reassured us that such catastrophes belong to the past, not to our future.

There's just one problem. It doesn't work. Because we know that secularism didn't deliver us from evil. Because we're still traumatized in the West by what that war drew out of us, what that war revealed in us. We have yet to heal.

3. Michael Horton, *Shaman and Sage: The Roots of the "Spiritual but Not Religious" in Antiquity* (Grand Rapids: Eerdmans, 2024).
4. Heiko A. Oberman, *Luther: Man Between God and the Devil* (New Haven, CT: Yale University Press, 1982).
5. Jim Davis and Michael Graham, with Ryan Burge, *The Great Dechurching: Who's Leaving, Why Are They Going, and What Will It Take to Bring Them Back?* (Grand Rapids: Zondervan Reflective, 2023).
6. Alec Ryrie, *Unbelievers: An Emotional History of Doubt* (Cambridge, MA: Belknap, 2019).

Narrow Road

You see that longing for healing in books, fiction and nonfiction, written by authors who never even experienced Japanese prison camps. Richard Flanagan's *The Narrow Road to the Deep North* won the Man Booker Prize in 2014 for best English-language fiction published in the United Kingdom or Ireland. Flanagan, who lives in Tasmania, introduces us to Australian war hero Dorrigo Evans, a doctor who endured unimaginable horror while helping construct the Burma Railway. Evans becomes a beloved national celebrity but can't shake his experience of slavery. The accounts are so brutal they could give readers nightmares today.

The Narrow Road to the Deep North is a survival story where the main characters die, a love story that celebrates infidelity, a hero story that valorizes duty and ends in tragedy. It's a story we expect to end well but concludes with no peace, with no hope. "He would live in hell," Flanagan writes, "because love is that also."[7] Flanagan captures the mood of Western despair: "He was a lighthouse whose light could not be relit. In his dreams he could hear his mother calling to him from the kitchen: Boy, come here, boy. But when he would go inside it was dark and cold, the kitchen was charred beams and ash and smelt of gas, and no one was home."[8]

Contrast Flanagan's award-winning novel with Laura Hillenbrand's 2010 international bestseller with the defiant title *Unbroken: A World War II Story of Survival, Resilience, and Redemption*.[9] Capturing a more American spirit, Hillenbrand tells the real-life story of Olympic athlete Louis Zamperini, who survived not only the Japanese prison camps but also forty-seven days of typhoons and shark attacks while floating in the Pacific Ocean.

7. Richard Flanagan, *The Narrow Road to the Deep North* (New York: Vintage, 2013), 353.
8. Flanagan, *Narrow Road to the Deep North*, 352.
9. Laura Hillenbrand, *Unbroken: A World War II Story of Survival, Resilience, and Redemption* (New York: Random House, 2010).

Zamperini, whose story became a feature film directed by Angelina Jolie in 2014, returned home and married his wife in 1946.

But Hillenbrand's title gets the story exactly wrong. Zamperini returned home broken. Traumatized by the war, he became an alcoholic and abused his pregnant wife, who sought a divorce. Unbroken, he was not.

But the West is broken. Traumatized by knowing the evils we could commit. Traumatized by knowing what evils could be committed against us and the ones we love. Convinced Christ offers no consolation, weakly trying to reassure ourselves that Hitler belongs to the past, yet broken by the weight of the world, knowing our lighthouse has gone out. It's dark and cold, and no one's home.

That's where Evans's story ends in fiction. But it's not where Zamperini's story ended in real life. The weight of his sin led him to seek help. In 1949 he attended the historic Billy Graham evangelistic meetings in Los Angeles. After Zamperini professed faith in Jesus Christ, the spiritual transformation was so complete that he forgave his Japanese captors. He threw away his alcohol. His nightmares ended. Their marriage survived until his wife died in 2001. And Zamperini shone the light of Christ until he died in 2014 at ninety-seven years old.

In cultural apologetics we don't shy away from hard questions about Christian failures, as in World War II. Heroes like Dietrich Bonhoeffer were the exception, not the rule, in standing against evil. But we don't shy away from asking hard questions about secularism either. In the traumatic aftermath of this war that claimed tens of millions of lives, how can we integrate individual freedom with collective responsibility? How many like the fictional Evans have failed to find freedom through hedonic numbing? Against the repressive collective ideas of communism and fascism, could Christianity retain individual identity while still encouraging collective peace through forgiveness, as with Zamperini toward his captors?

The biggest failure of secularism is the inability to integrate the individual with the collective. The Second World War damned the collective, including the church, to the point of eliminating any purpose for our individual freedoms in the West today. This is the loss of narrative that makes shared action feel impossible. We have unprecedented freedom and prosperity, in large part thanks to the sacrifices of our ancestors in World War II. But we have no good use for it. No one's home. All that's left are the charred beams and ash of a civilization largely forgotten.

In the cultural apologetics showcased by this book, we hope to reawaken the memory of Christianity and the hope of a new heaven and new earth to come with Christ. Cultural apologetics helps Christians share the truth, goodness, and beauty of the gospel as the only hope that fulfills our deepest longings. And our deepest longing is personal peace with God that results in collective peace with each other. That longing leads to Calvary and the man who is the very Son of God hanging for love on a horizontal beam grounded by a vertical beam. At this crossroads for the West, take the narrow, well-worn road to Emmaus. Follow the risen one who can be found in all the Scriptures (Luke 24:27).

Scripture Index

Subject Index

Timothy Keller

His Spiritual and Intellectual Formation

The untold story of the people, the books, the lectures, and ultimately the God who formed and shaped the life of the late Timothy Keller.

Millions have read books and listened to sermons by Timothy Keller. But who impacted his own thinking, and what shaped his spiritual growth and ministry priorities? With full access to Keller's personal notes and sermons—as well as exclusive interviews with family members and longtime friends—Collin Hansen takes readers behind the scenes of one of the 21st century's most influential church leaders.

For the first time, Hansen introduces readers to Keller's early years: the home where he learned to tell stories from the trees, the church where he learned to care for souls, and the city that lifted him to the international fame he never wanted.

This unique biography will allow you to:

- Understand the principles and practices that allowed Keller to synthesize so many different influences in a coherent ministry.
- Take the best of Keller's preaching and teaching to meet emerging challenges in the twenty-first century.
- Develop your own historical, theological, and cultural perspectives to shape your leadership.

The story of Timothy Keller is the story of his spiritual and intellectual influences, from the woman who taught him how to read the Bible to the professor who taught him to preach Jesus from every text to the philosopher who taught him to see beneath society's surface.

The Keller Center
for CULTURAL APOLOGETICS

The Keller Center for Cultural Apologetics helps Christians share the truth, goodness, and beauty of the gospel as the only hope that fulfills our deepest longings.

Learn more:

www.thekellercenter.org